SDI Rescue Diving Manual

A Guide to Rescue Techniques, Stress, Injury, and Accident Management

by
Joe Mokry

SCUBA DIVING
INTERNATIONAL

Published by
International Training, Inc.
Topsham, Maine

SDI Rescue Diving Manual: A Guide to Rescue Techniques, Stress, Injury, and Accident Management
by Joe Mokry

Scuba Diving International
18 Elm Street
Topsham, ME 04086
Tel: 207-729-4201
FAX: 207-729-4453

Find us on the World Wide Web at http://www.tdisdi.com/

© 2001 International Training, Inc.

Photography
Cover and Principal photography by Bret Gilliam. ©Bret Gilliam. All rights reserved.
Other photographs by Steven M. Barsky, Joe Mokry, and Wayne Hasson.
Primary photo models: Lance DeRoche, Cathryn Castle, Gretchen Gilliam, Lynn Hendrickson, Joe Mokry, Scott Lockwood, Jill Haines, Brian Carney, John Kooistra, Tanya Burnett, and David Sipperly.
Layout and design by Steven M. Barsky, Marine Marketing and Consulting

Illustrations:
© Steven M. Barsky. All rights reserved.

Printed by Ojai Printing, Ojai, CA

ISBN Number: 1-931451-02-8

Library of Congress Control Number: 2001089040

Other Titles Available from Scuba Diving International

Training Manual for Scuba Diving: Dive Training for the 21st Century
Easy Nitrox Diving
Night Diving, Underwater Navigation and Limited Visibility Diving
Deeper Diving with Dive Computers
Wreck Diving and Boat Diving Techniques
Dry Suit Diving
Solo Diving Techniques: A Manual for Independent Diving Skills
Visual Inspection Procedures: A Manual for Cylinder Safety
CPROX: Guidelines for Essential CPR and Oxygen Administration
CPR-FIRST: A Concise Manual for Emergency First Aid and CPR

Other Titles Available from Technical Diving International

Nitrox Diver Manual
Advanced Nitrox Diver Manual
Decompression Procedures
Semi-Closed Circuit Rebreather Manual: Draeger Units
Trimix Diving Manual
Extended Range Diver Manual
Cave and Cavern Diving Manual
Advanced Wreck Diving
Deep Diving: An Advanced Guide to Physiology, Procedures, and Systems
Nitrox Blending Manual: Guide to Preparation of Oxygen Enriched Air
Advanced Gas Blending Manual: Nitrox, Trimix, and Custom Mixes

Table of Contents

Table of Contents

Table of Contents

Foreword

Bret Gilliam, CEO Scuba Diving Intnl.

It's often said that the best life-guards don't have to make any rescues. A true professional can recognize an accident or stress scenario before it happens and intervene with positive results.

While diving is generally conducted in a fairly benign setting, the marine environment can be a hostile, unforgiving place. Inevitably, what can go wrong, will go wrong for some people. How you deal with these situations can mean the difference between a learned response to stress that neutralizes the situation or allows it to escalate into a lesson in survival.

There's not much mystery about sport diving and the scenarios for accidents are predictable and manageable for the most part. This book is dedicated to providing information to help you learn confident independent diver skills as well as giving you the tools to help others. A large part of preventing stressful problems and accidents is developing an awareness as a diver to potential scenarios and taking early action to eliminate rescue situations.

Joe Mokry, a top rescue professional, is our author for this text because of his pioneering work in diving and boat rescue. Joe has trained police, fire, and U.S. Coast Guard teams in all phases of water rescue as well as working with divers of all levels. His no nonsense approach to the subject brings a career perspective of unequalled experience and application under varying conditions. He is well respected in his field.

This book will help you "dive defensively" and provide the educational basis for skills for self-rescue and the rescue of others. Study the information contained in this valuable resource and practice both the mental and physical skills to proficiency. Some day, maybe sooner than you think, you'll need them.

Bret Gilliam, President & CEO, SCUBA DIVING INTERNATIONAL

Chapter 1
Safe Diving
and the Diver

The Self-Reliant Diver

Your view of scuba diving has probably changed somewhat from the time of your initial training program to the time when you're ready to undertake rescue diver training. You've broadened your range of experience through repeated diving activities in increasingly wider types of diving environments. You've learned new skills, "tricks of the trade", amassed more knowledge, and dived with several, if not many, buddies. You've gained experience and judgment, the two indispensable keys to safer, more enjoyable diving. Most of your beginner's jitters and reservations have been conquered and you feel that you're becoming the kind of diver you always wanted to be; reliable, capable and self-reliant. Self-reliant?

Self-reliance is as important an attribute as a diver can possess. If you haven't given this much thought before, this would be a good time to do so. Admittedly, the ability to look after all your problems underwater without assistance from a buddy may not be the first thing that would occur to you when you consider what you need to dive properly. After all, the point was made time and time again in your training programs that you always dive with a buddy. This is a good rule that helps increase your enjoyment of diving, brings people together in a shared social setting and gives you the confidence to explore new areas. So, where does self-reliance come in?

Imagine for a moment that you and your buddy are nearing the end of what has been a truly memorable dive: the walls were vertical and blanketed in the kinds of marine life seen only in the magazines, the warm water was clear enough to see from here to next week, and the prospect of relating the dive to envious friends back home beckons. Then you realize that your buddy is gone. Which of you is responsible for this: you, because you were daydreaming, or your buddy, because he stopped to take just one more photograph? Your own air supply is dwindling and you suspect that your buddy may have even less. It dawns on you that you're not even sure where you are; you weren't paying that much attention on the way back, and your buddy was doing the navigating anyway. What to do?

Looking around more carefully, you see bubbles in the distance and swim to your buddy who's trying hard to tighten a loose weight belt while balancing the camera and the demands of buoyancy control at the same time. With a little help from you the crisis is quickly resolved and you're both soon back on the boat again and reliving the highpoints of the dive. Some new lessons have been learned, too. Never again will you leave the navigation entirely in someone else's hands, and you wish to seek out a buddy who is independently capable of looking after typical underwater problems without causing you moments of anxious concern.

TDI/SDI believes that all divers should be trained to be self-sufficient. This means that each diver accepts the responsibility for his or her own planning, equipment and performance underwater. We are all ultimately responsible for our own safety and conduct on a dive. Any time our problems require assistance from our buddy on a dive, we disrupt the flow of the dive at the least and possibly endanger them at the worst. In fact what we strive to be is the ideal buddy; able to plan and lead the dive, capable of looking after most underwater problems, attentive and responsible. We can become better than we are by practicing and refining the basic skills of diving and by

Relaxed confidence is a characteristic of the self-reliant diver.

developing new skills and knowledge. Many of the new assessment and problem solving skills that will make you an independently capable diver will be learned in this Rescue Diver course. Along with this will come the knowledge that you'll also become a more valuable dive buddy.

Self-Reliance
- **Understand your equipment**
- **Take personal responsibility**
- **Develop self-awareness skills**
- **Become more aware of your surroundings**
- **Plan for contingencies**
- **Learn to handle your own emergencies**

Awareness

Self-awareness to a diver means keeping in touch with the personal factors affecting our survival underwater. These include how cold or tired we are, how we and our equipment, as a system, are working together, and knowing what our remaining air and actual depth are at any given moment without having to look at the gauges. While this may all seem obvious, it's common enough for divers to withdraw from their surroundings and forget to pay attention to what's happening to them. This is not a diver in the comfort zone. This is also a diver more likely to blunder into an accident simply from carelessness.

"Global awareness" is defined as attentiveness to our surroundings, and is equally important in staying out of trouble underwater. In practice it gives us the ability to "feel" in a 3-dimensional sense. An alert diver knows his orientation underwater, maintains his sense of direction at all times and in his mind's eye "sees" himself in the middle of a changing seascape as he fins through the water. Global-awareness helps you register approaching entanglements and evade them, judge distances from the bottom and avoid kicking up the silt, stay in synchronous motion with a buddy without getting in the way and almost instinctively pick the best natural navigation clues. It's no coincidence that both self-awareness and global-awareness are the hallmarks of the self-reliant diver.

Dives are always more enjoyable when each diver is independently competent.

Preparing for the dive

Most of us view diving as a liberating experience that frees us from our every-day "topside" worries. Still, preparation in advance of the dive will help ensure that we make the most our time underwater, and do so enjoyably. These activities fall into several categories.

Physical Preparation

Scuba diving is a relaxing activity, one that allows the neutrally buoyant diver to swim with little effort and to stop and rest underwater whenever the diver feels the need. Nevertheless, the presence of currents and surge underwater can significantly increase the diver's workload. Gearing up on the boat or on shore and entering the water wearing 60 to 100 lbs. of equipment can be physically demanding. Exiting the water after a long swim to shore or the dive boat can exhaust an already tired diver. In short, despite our view that diving is effortless, we can expend a great deal of energy on almost any dive. Add to this the caloric requirements to stay warm in anything but the most tropical waters and it's evident that even "easy" dives are work.

With this in mind, divers should strive to maintain a level of fitness appropriate to their typical kinds of diving. For all of us, we should attempt at the least to undertake sufficient regular exercise to keep us in condition for diving. This should include regular swimming sessions, especially with mask, snorkel and fins. Any other exercises that emphasize cardiovascular fitness such as, running, tennis, and most competitive sports will also provide benefit for divers.

Keep in mind that many of the rescue skills and techniques you will be performing in TDI/SDI's Rescue Diver program will require sustained physical effort. Real life rescues may involve a long towing assist of a tired buddy. Even minimal swims on the surface while towing a helpless person can be exhausting. Are you ready?

Mental Preparation

A sure way to avoid pre-dive jitters is good mental preparation for the dive. If it's a site that's new to you, this starts with having done adequate research in advance of the dive. Talk to divers who have done the dive before, study the charts for the area, learn where all the entry and exit points are, and understand the effects of weather on the dive site. If the dive is challenging, such as boat diving on a relatively deep wreck, this might be a good time to review your present experience and training to make an honest determination as to whether you're really ready for this type of dive.

If you think you're up to the challenge and are diving in solid, experienced company, then you might benefit from mentally walking through the proposed dive with your dive buddy. Examine each step of the dive process to familiarize yourself with the way it should all unfold. Then mentally create some of the possible obstructions to the smooth progress of your dive. This kind of preparation will help prepare you for the many unforeseen events that so often arise in even the most straightforward dives.

Equipment Preparation

Scuba diving is an equipment-intensive activity. Without properly functioning dive gear, we run the risk of equipment malfunction while underwater, particularly during deep or high-exertion activities. Equipment preparation, however, extends even to our exposure suit. Improperly cared for suits may get stiff and uncomfortable with age. The same may happen to improperly cared for bodies. If it's been a while since you last had the suit on, good advanced preparation would call for a pre-dive fitting to ensure that the suit is still serviceable.

Regular annual inspection and maintenance of all scuba equipment, including regulator, buoyancy compensator, and air cylinders will help prevent avoidable gear breakdowns that may cut a dive short, or cause an underwater emergency. Make sure that all your underwater gauges are in good working order. Check electrical contacts on bottom timers and computers. These need to be kept clean and without corrosion to function reliably during the dive. TDI/SDI believe that dive computers are an essential component to good diving. A computer that fails during a dive calls for an immediate end to the dive. You will not probably be near decompression limits on any average dive; however, always remember to make a safety stop at 15 ft (5 m) for at least three minutes on ascent. The use of a marked descent line and alternate timer will allow a proper stop in the event of computer failure.

Specialized equipment required for the upcoming dive should be inspected well in advance. This might include line reels, lift bags, bottom grid lines for plotting debris or artifact distribution, marking buoys and flags, inflatable personal markers and the batteries in underwater cameras, strobes and dive lights. The last thing you should have to worry about is whether your dive gear is going to be able to perform as well as you will on the dive.

Dive Planning

Few pre-dive activities are more important than setting up a good *agreed-on* dive plan. All divers in the group or both divers in a buddy pair should participate. The dive intentions and nature should be clearly stated to avoid confusion later on. The dive plan should include the maximum depth and time of the dive and be calculated to keep all divers out of mandatory decompression time or if decompression stops are planned, that sufficient cylinders are in place. Most experienced divers will already have a good working number for their air consumption rate, and this should be compared to the proposed maximum depth and time of the dive. Be sure to allow adequate reserve air for the safety stop at 15 ft (3 m) for three minutes, as well as sufficient air for emergency use.

The dive plan will also include a proposed route to follow underwater. This provides for a much better sense of orientation during the dive, as the divers should be able to visualize their relative position on the route at any time. Deviations from the route are always acceptable as long as both divers

Continued training increases both your skill level and experience.

Diving Hand Signals

Stop	*Something is wrong*	*OK?,OK*	*OK?,OK (gloved)*
Go up, going up	*Go down, going down*	*Which direction?*	*Get with your buddy*
You lead, I'll follow	*Level off, this depth*		*Take it easy, slow down*
Distress, help!	*OK? OK (on surface at distance)*		*OK?OK (one hand occupied)*
Come here	*Me, or watch me*	*Out of air*	*Buddy breathe or share air*
Danger	*Ears not clearing*	*I am cold*	*Go that way*

understand and agree to the changes. The route should be designed to bring the divers back to their entry point, or another selected alternative.

All divers and surface support personnel should review the range of hand signals that might be used on the dive. This is best done before the divers are fully geared up for the dive and are impatient to get into the water. This review should include the support personnel as well, as hand signals may be used for communication to them from divers on the surface.

Buddy Check

One of the most important ways to ensure a successful dive and to avert accidents is to get in the habit of conducting a thorough buddy check before every dive. Most divers start with checking the scuba unit and air supply. Ensure that straps on the harness or buoyancy compensator are not twisted and are properly buckled. Typically the second stage of the regulator will come over the diver's right shoulder, though this is not always the case with some models. This is a good time to make note of this fact, as it will change your mutual orientation if buddy breathing should become necessary. Note also the arrangement of your buddy's octopus or other backup air supply. Be sure you know precisely where to find it in an out-of-air situation. Ideally the octopus will be distinctly colored and attached in such a way that it can be quickly released.

Complete your check of the scuba unit by noting your buddy's starting air pressure and that any gauge and dive computer are in good condition and functional. A quick test to determine whether the air supply has been fully turned on is to hold the pressure gauge in one hand while pressing the purge button on the second stage. The needle on the gauge should not move.

Continue the buddy check by examining the mask and snorkel, ensuring

Buddy Check
• Is air on? Alternate air source?
• Are all hoses properly placed?
• Is mask sealed? Are straps secure?
• Weight system release accessible?
• Dive knife or tool in place?
• Signal review?
• Dive plan review?
• Contingencies review?

that the hood does not lift the mask and that all straps are in place. Pay particular attention to the weight belt or other integrated weighting system. The buckle on the belt must be unobstructed by any other straps or belts and readily accessible. Pull-toggles or any other mechanism used to release integrated weights must be both properly functioning and completely understood by both divers. There should be no doubt about how to drop the weight in an emergency situation. Take this opportunity as well to check that the belt, if used, is snug around your buddy. One frequent cause of inability to release a belt when necessary is that the belt loosens in the water and swings around so that the buckle is behind the diver. It may be almost impossible to reach the release mechanism without removing the diver's buoyancy compensator and scuba unit first in these cases. Remember that it is almost always a mistake to remove a diver's buoyancy source before dropping his ballast.

Note where your buddy's straps are on the dive knife or other tool. Most frequently this will be on the lower leg. The general recommendation is that the tool be strapped inside the calf so that a dropped weight belt doesn't get snagged while falling. Many divers, especially those frequently involved in rescue operations, will wear a second knife, often placed within easy reach on the buoyancy compensator. In some circumstances, such as walk-in entries on rocky beaches, dive fins will not be put on until the divers are in the water. In any case offer assistance to your buddy in donning fins. Make sure straps are straight and properly placed.

It should go without saying that all these steps of checking your buddy before entering the water apply to you as well. Take the time needed to familiarize your buddy with the configuration of your own gear. You may be the one to require assistance on the dive, and your buddy may be the one who will have to handle the emergency, including your equipment.

Special Emergency Skills

Beyond the specialized rescue skills you will learn in the Rescue Diver course, there are particular diving skills that will both increase your safety and improve your effectiveness during emergency situations. While these are skills that any competent diver should possess, the nature of distress on or under the water calls for refined abilities to deal with emergencies.

Out-of-Air Emergencies

Most divers will gratefully spend their diving careers without ever having to face the prospect of an out-of-air emergency underwater. Proper dive planning, prudent air rationing and staying within bottom time limits will diminish that possibility even more. Nevertheless, circumstances will sometimes conspire against us and result in air shortage situations. This can happen by not leaving enough air for a full safety stop, deviating from the planned route that results in extended swims back to the exit point, "lost buddy" searches, unanticipated currents on the way back, stopping to relieve cramps and delays due to entanglements. Fighting for breath as the pressure gauge shows very low air pressure can be panic inducing. Reviewing your options before this happens is only good emergency preparation. There may be more choices available than you think.

Buddy Dependent Options

The most widely employed option for the diver in a low air situation is to "borrow" air from his buddy. Always remember that if you are out of air, or nearly so, that your buddy is likely in the same or similar situation. At worst this makes the buddy dependent option one that exposes both of you to the risk of an out-of-air problem. At best it's a solution that calls for an immediate ascent together to the surface.

The preferred method of sharing air is through the use of an octopus regulator or other additional second stage (sometimes referred to as a "safe second"). There are several variations of second stage regulators directly incorporated into the low-pressure inflator hose. In both cases the mouthpiece/second stage must be cleared or purged before inhaling a full breath. Whatever the arrangement, the out-of-air diver should know exactly where to find and how to use the device. This is a critical part of the buddy check and should never be left until the time of need.

Procedure for using an octopus regulator
1. The out-of-air diver signals "out of air" and "share air".
2. The air donor passes over the octopus regulator or allows receiving diver to take it from him.
3. Both divers grasp each other's buoyancy compensator or harness straps with their right hands.
4. Maintaining constant eye contact, the divers ascend together, using their left hands to vent air from their buoyancy devices as required.
5. Keep breathing as regular and normal as possible during this ascent.
6. On the surface both divers make themselves buoyant.

Buddy breathing, or sharing a single second stage, has been used successfully many times to assist an out-of-air diver. This method has been largely

An octopus regulator is the preferred buddy-dependent option.

replaced by required training in the use of an octopus regulator. All TDI/SDI training requires an octopus, though buddy breathing remains an effective alternative, *but only if practiced on a regular basis.* Any out-of-air emergency is a stressful event and to employ buddy breathing as the alternative of choice will necessitate that the divers exercise excellent self control, thus the need for frequent practice.

Procedure for buddy breathing

1. The out-of-diver signals "out of air" and "share air".
2. The air donor takes a breath before passing the second stage to the receiver.
3. The receiving diver guides the regulator to his mouth and takes two breaths.
4. The donor replaces the regulator and takes two breaths in turn before passing it back to the receiver.
5. Throughout this exchange the divers hold on to each other, the receiver using his right hand to grasp the donor's BC, while the donor uses his left hand to grasp the receiver's BC. The donor uses his right hand to pass the regulator while the receiver uses his left hand to guide the regulator to his mouth.
6. Be sure that both divers exhale slightly whenever the regulator is not in their mouth.
7. Both divers ascend carefully together, venting air from their buoyancy compensators as required.

Buddy Independent Options

Both buddy breathing and using a buddy's octopus share the drawback of requiring that your buddy be nearby, be practiced in the proper techniques and that the urgency of the situation does not cause mistakes. The best options are those that allow the out-of-air diver to act independently to help himself. These fall into two categories: redundant air supplies, and direct ascents.

Redundant air supplies

Probably the most useful and easiest method of solving an out-of-air problem is to have a true alternate air source. A completely redundant system would include tank and regulator. This has the further advantage of a replacement regulator if in fact the out-of-air emergency is actually caused by a faulty regulator, rather than an empty scuba cylinder. Typically called "pony bottles," these small tank setups range in size from as little as 6 cubic feet to 40 cubic feet capacity. The most commonly used sizes are the 13 and 19 cubic foot bottles. Depending on the depth, pony bottles will allow a diver several to many minutes of bottom time, usually more than enough to ascend safely to the surface.

Increasingly popular among serious sport divers are self-contained bottle and integrated regulator devices, such as Spare Air® and its smaller relative HEEDS. The latter is essentially an escape air supply for pilots or others who may be temporarily entrapped underwater. Spare Air® also provides a short-term air supply, though with its larger size (up to almost 2 ft^3), it gives the diver a little more ascent time. Both units have a built-in regulator with mouthpiece and are refillable from scuba cylinders.

Whether having a pony bottle or small, integrated bottle/regulator system available in emergencies, the diver is still in need of refresher practice from time to time. You need to be completely certain of where to find the second stage of the pony bottle regulator or the holster holding the Spare Air without thinking about it. Bear in mind that if you were wearing certain types of full-face masks when you ran out of air, then you will also be mask-less when you ditch your regulator for an alternate air source. It might be advisable to carry a spare mask in a side pocket for this possibility.

Direct ascent

Often times it may be quicker and easier to ascend directly to the surface without pausing to change air supplies, signal your buddy to share air or otherwise delay. Certainly in depths of less than 30 ft. (9 m), the surface is only seconds away. Considering the time it might take to employ another option,

A true alternate air source is usually the best option in an out-of-air emergency.

a direct ascent might make more sense with less risk to either diver. There are several important points to keep in mind, however, to make this a successful procedure.

First, even though you may not be able to get a breath from the regulator at 40', it's unlikely that the cylinder is completely empty, even if the regulator had been free flowing. Most likely there is simply insufficient pressure left to overcome the ambient pressure due to the depth. This means that as you rise in the water and the ambient pressure falls, there should be some residue of air in the tank available to you. The shallower you ascend, the more air is available. Clearly, to take advantage of this air, you must have your regulator in place. The procedure, then, is to attempt to inhale on ascent, to exhale normally, and to attempt to inhale. As long as you continue to attempt to inhale and exhale normally, your airway will stay open and any expanding air will automatically vent from your lungs on its own. This will happen even as you attempt to inhale.

As you get to shallower water, you'll find that you'll get as much air as you need (when you really need it). Remember, *never* hold your breath on ascent. Methods that limit your exhalation such as humming, blowing a fine stream of bubbles, etc., will likely cause some lung expansion. The surest way to avoid a lung over-expansion problem is to keep the airway open by attempting to breathe normally throughout the ascent.

Limited Visibility

Diving in conditions of visibility less than 5 ft. (1.5 m) will often lead the buddy pair into problems of separation and navigation. Separation of buddies during a dive is not an unusual event, but may become more than a nuisance if conditions are unfavorable to rapidly finding the other. Prevention is the best cure in this case. Agree beforehand that you and your buddy will stay within arm's length throughout the dive and will frequently check with each other. Determine who will lead the dive so that the other is not jostling to be in front. In severely limited conditions a buddy line, i.e., a 6 ft. (2 m) length of line held between the divers, will be necessary to maintain constant contact.

Despite your best efforts, however, buddies will inevitably drift apart on occasion. This is not in itself an emergency, but the stress level in both divers is sure to rise if they cannot readily find each other. As long as both divers understand and apply the same "lost buddy search", then the separation will last only a minute or two. This may be an anxious time in some circumstances, but rarely will divers fail to be reunited shortly if they follow the same plan.

In low visibility conditions, divers might consider using a buddy line between them.

Lost buddy search

1. As soon as you realize that your buddy is gone, stop and take a good look around you, looking up and down as well as from side to side.

2. It helps to rise a few feet when you survey the area around you. If your buddy has stayed at the same depth, you may see the reflection of light off the tops of his bubbles.

3. Spend no more than about a minute looking for your buddy. It may help to backtrack a bit to determine if he stopped for some reason, rather than wandered off on his own.

4. Ascend to the surface, always observing the correct ascent rates and procedures.

5. If not already there looking for you, your buddy should arrive shortly.

6. If your buddy has not returned to the surface after 5 minutes, there may indeed be a problem and you should consider calling for assistance.

Most experienced divers go to some lengths to prevent this kind of situation from happening at all. Surfacing and returning to depth is not only a waste of time and air, but also makes divers more prone to precipitate decompression sickness. It also causes "wear and tear" on the ears and sinuses due to repeated, and unnecessary, pressure changes.

Navigation

Limited visibility diving is essentially a test of a diver's self control and ability. There will always be a certain amount of stress associated with diving in poor visibility conditions. Divers prefer to have readily available visual reference points to help them plot their course across an otherwise featureless bottom. In the case of visibility of less than about 5 ft. (1.5 m), divers are forced to conduct all their wayfinding through the use of their instruments, particularly the compass.

Good navigational skills are essential to any kind of diving activity, but are often neglected by divers. Diving in clear visibility waters, having readily apparent underwater landmarks or being routinely guided by other divers, it is easy to become lazy in wayfinding skills. Planning a search for a missing diver and actually conducting such a search will usually require that we possess fairly refined navigational skills. Most search patterns that we might undertake will necessitate that we can cover the bottom in an organized and

Every diver should be accomplished in the art of accurate underwater navigation.

systematic fashion. This demands skills that will guarantee our being able to conduct the search and not get lost ourselves.

As with any other diving skill, we lose proficiency when we fail to practice. Get into the habit of using a compass on every dive. Set up your dive plans so that they require some facility with navigational ability to complete them. Challenge yourself by making the compass critical to completing underwater routes successfully. Certain standard search patterns, as discussed later, will depend on these skills.

Even more importantly, the rescue diver should become adept at the

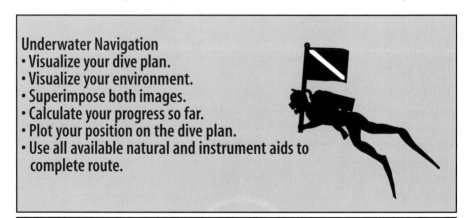

Underwater Navigation
- Visualize your dive plan.
- Visualize your environment.
- Superimpose both images.
- Calculate your progress so far.
- Plot your position on the dive plan.
- Use all available natural and instrument aids to complete route.

skills of global awareness. Place yourself in your environment and know where you are at all times. There is a multitude of clues available on almost every dive. Learn to visualize your plan and route, and you'll begin to feel orientated throughout the dive.

Scuba I.Q. Review

1. What does the term "self-reliant" diver mean?

2. A diver's sense of awareness underwater is made up of what two components?

3. List three essential parts of a good dive plan.

4. What two broad categories of options describe responses to out-of-air emergencies?

5. When might a diver favor a buddy-independent response to a buddy-dependent response in an out-of-air emergency?

6. Describe two self-rescue options for an out-of-air diver at a depth of 20' (6 m).

Chapter 2
How Stress Leads to Diving Emergencies

Stress in Diving

Most of us became involved in scuba diving because we were attracted by the ideas of exploring the hidden underwater world with its shipwrecks and marine life, traveling to warm, clear water tropical dive sites, and enjoying the weightless sensation and extended bottom time that breath-hold diving doesn't offer. For most of us, too, scuba diving both promised and delivered on all this. The heart of the attraction to diving is adventure, the never knowing exactly what you'll see or precisely where you'll go or how your dive plan will play itself out. It's also fair to say that adventure is some combination of uncertainty, moderate thrills and the unexpected. All this, to a large extent, is the reason we learned to dive and why we continue to dive.

The same components of adventure are also sources of stress in divers. Divers in training and newly-certified divers are particularly prone to bouts of stress before open water dives. Hollywood depiction of underwater terrors, wildly-exaggerated stories from veteran divers and the sure knowledge that spending any amount of time underwater without coming up for air is just unnatural, all conspire to raise the stress level of the novice. A large part of the diving instructor's role, in fact, is in creating a comfort level that induces eagerness rather than anxiety and confidence rather than bravado in the student. Still, many novice divers will enter the water with the thought that

Scuba diving is an adventure, but may also produce anxiety and apprehension.

they will always be waging a life-or-death battle with hypothermia, malicious currents and insatiable predators. Stress is a predictable consequence of this train of thought.

While experience soon teaches us that our fears are a poor reflection of reality, any diver can be overtaken by gnawing concerns in the right circumstances. A veteran freshwater diver may be intimidated by the seemingly endless expanse of ocean. An ocean diver may be unprepared for the extra care required not to stir up the bottom in most lakes and thus be caught unawares by the suddenly limited visibility. Certainly any diver not specifically trained for overhead environments such as penetration wreck diving or ice diving will quail at the prospect, and probably should, if the diver's buddy attempts or proposes this kind of activity.

The diving environment itself, which may include cold water, choppy surface conditions and, perhaps, the diver's first night dive, can mentally and psychologically tax any diver not used to these circumstances. Again, stress will be a natural consequence of this train of thought. Adventure now becomes a mix rather heavier on the uncertainty and unexpected side, and lighter on the moderate thrill side. Furthermore, left to its own devices, the mind's eye has little difficulty in conjuring up escalating levels of potential drama that may ultimately result in its owner's inability to make rational choices. In short a stressed diver may be in trouble before even entering the water.

Recognizing Stress in Others

A certain amount of stress will almost always accompany a diver in preparation for a dive. The mental state that sets this ball rolling will also be unlikely to improve by itself as time goes on. The truth is that stressed divers tend to become more anxious as time passes and the prospect of the dive comes nearer.

We need to be able recognize undue anxiety when we see it in others and take corrective action sooner rather than later. A few appropriate words early on may prevent a very difficult situation later. Stressed divers may show their true feelings about a diving situation in several ways.

Withdrawal

Preyed upon by fears of the impending dive, some divers will 'freeze up" and withdraw from the flow of conversation around them. They may become uncommunicative and seek a more private place away from others who may be chatting excitedly about the dive plan. When asked to offer an opinion on the plan such as where to enter or what route to follow, the diver may reply with an unconvincing, "I don't care." This reply is probably a long way from the truth, but the fact is that the diver simply can't or doesn't want to deal with the realities of the proposed dive. Perhaps intimidated by the ebullience around him and not wanting to be the one to "spoil" everyone else's adventure, the diver increasingly withdraws from the group.

Apprehension about an upcoming dive may cause some divers to withdraw from the activity around them.

The dive scene, whether on board a boat or beach, can be a busy place with several buddy pairs, a dive recorder, a Divemaster, friends and family and others in attendance. Amid all this activity, it takes a perceptive buddy to pick up the suddenly quiet mood of the stressed diver and to recognize it for what it means.

Recognizing the Signs of Stress
- Withdrawal
- Hyperactivity
- Constant talking
- Gear fumbling
- Inappropriate or "black" humor
- Moodiness

Gear Problems

A diver uncertain about his ability to undertake a particular dive, distracted by personal concerns unrelated to the dive, or just not "up" to it today will find many excuses to delay entry into the water. Among the most common are gear-related "problems". A broken fin strap, a leaky "O" ring, a minute hole in a glove all become reasons to abort the day's activities and go home. Often, too, a stressed diver will improperly assemble the scuba unit or appear confused about the correct assembly procedure. It helps to know the diver well enough to tell whether or not he is stalling or simply a confused, poorly trained diver. Bear in mind, however, that any diver making so many mistakes or having so many excuses will probably not make the safest of buddies anyway. A little pre-dive counseling may allow the diver the way out he needs or straighten out the concerns he has before things go wrong underwater.

Hyperactivity or talking

Sometimes an apprehensive diver will mask fear or deep concerns in a false enthusiasm at odds with their usual calm, deliberate manner. Non-stop talking about nothing in particular or frequently repeating or re-phrasing the same topic will also alert the attentive buddy to an underlying problem. Early recognition of nervousness as the cause of this unusual behavior and gentle intervention to ease the diver's mind will often resolve problems before they become emergencies later.

Recognizing Stress in Yourself

All divers have experienced the sensation of apprehension prior to a dive. A dive in a new area, an unfamiliar wreck site, or a more complex than usual dive plan may all cause us anxiety before the dive. Even a dive in familiar surroundings may take on more significance if sea state or other weather conditions are threatening or unusual. Often these feelings are just common-sense cautionary indications that call for extra vigilance to avoid complications. After all, experience will have shown us that compensating for the unexpected or unusual is only prudent. Still, fear that you may have overlooked something in your planning is not the same as that nagging reluctance to perform the activity at all. The lure that pulls us to go ahead with the dive may be counteracted by the apprehension that pushes us away. This push-pull results in a stress level that may make us a threat to our own safety and a burden to our buddy.

In this kind of situation, there is no substitute for an honest self-examination. Ask yourself some questions that may help you define the specific

Stress may be caused by diving new and unfamiliar sites, by new activities such as night diving, or when diving with new dive buddies. Recognize stress in yourself and others before it becomes panic.

causes of your anxiety and face up to them. Is this an "experience expanding" activity, or am I significantly exceeding my training and prior experience? Do I have the skills to perform this dive safely? If things start going wrong underwater, am I really briefed and prepared for the contingencies? Am I capable of looking after myself and my buddy in an emergency under these conditions? If the answer is "No" to these questions, then maybe your fears are well grounded and this may not be the best time or circumstances to undertake the planned dive.

Very often, however, pre-dive concerns are more of a psychological nature than real. Fear of the unknown and fear of failure, especially in front of others, can shake our confidence even when the proposed dive is within our capabilities. Understanding this for what it is will help us achieve a mental state to deal with our concerns realistically.

Dealing with stress
Separate Fact from Fiction
This starts with a good dive plan. What exactly are the intentions of this dive? Have we decided on a firm route, air portioning and turn-around times? Are we clear on how to make changes to the plan underwater? Have we developed plans for contingencies such as unusual air consumption rates, earlier than planned surfacing or the possibility of having to make decompression stops before surfacing? A good dive plan ensures that you and everyone else involved understands exactly what is about to take place.

Conduct a Good Dive Briefing
A good dive briefing will not only cover the dive plan, but will also set up an organized response to emergencies. Knowing that everyone on scene has a pre-planned and designated role in emergency response can be a great comfort to any diver uncertain of their own ability to deal with complex

Maintaining active communication between buddies can help ease the tension a diver might feel about a dive.

problems single-handedly. Ensuring that this is carried out to our own satisfaction will also allay concerns that we, ourselves, might have. Be sure that the goals of the dive are well-understood. If you're unclear about something, don't hesitate to ask.

Conduct a Good Buddy Check

One of the best ways of catching accidents before they happen is to see to it that thorough buddy checks are always conducted before a dive. Loose gear, improperly secured weight belts, and twisted straps are just a few of the many problems that can be avoided by ensuring that all divers, including yourself, are "checked out" before entering the water. To be responsive in an emergency underwater, your buddy needs to be fully familiar with your equipment, as you need to be familiar with his. This awareness of the location and configuration of each other's equipment, as well as the familiarity of the buddy check routine, also has the result of reducing stress both in ourselves and in our buddy. Remember to include a review of signals, dive plan and out-of-air emergency procedures as part of the buddy check.

Talk to the Dive Leaders

Withdrawing from the activity around you isolates you from the input and clarifications you may need to feel comfortable with the dive. Confiding

The rewards of night diving include animals not often seen in the day and, very often, brilliant displays of phosphorescence.

Small incidents lead to other incidents and the situation can quickly snowball out of the control. For example, a diver making a loose weight belt a little more secure may lose track of his buoyancy and begin sinking. Pressure in the ears alerts him to his unplanned descent whereupon he adds air to the buoyancy compensator. Looking for an immediate response to his descent, he may well add too much air and thus find himself ascending more rapidly than is prudent. Any other complication added to this scenario, such as a mask leak, could be the trigger that drives this diver from frustrated and stressed to panic, and a too rapid ascent to the surface. Sometimes the line between stress and panic is a fine one.

Panicky Diver on the Surface

Panic on the surface is frequently caused by conditions that make it difficult for the diver to stay comfortably afloat, such as over-weighting. Inability to breathe easily will almost certainly induce a feeling of great stress and panic. This may be caused by a constricting wet or dry suit, a poorly maintained regulator, choppy sea state or alterations in breathing patterns from a general anxiety. A diver in this state wants desperately to be clear of the water, so will demonstrate some of the classic signs of water-induced panic; rapidly flailing arms and body as high as possible above the water, mask and regulator removed to ease breathing, gasping for breath and eyes wide open in fright.

**Dealing with stress in the water -
Act, don't just react!**
• **Stop where you are. Signal your buddy that
you have a problem.**
• **Take 2-3 full breaths to get your breathing
under control.**
• **Calm down and find the problem.**
• **Look at your options and make a rational choice.**

The panicky diver is, by definition, not rational and may pose a significant threat to any other diver within reach. In responding to a panicky diver, the buddy's first obligation is always to himself. Keeping out of reach until you've assessed the situation and decided on a course of action will keep you part of the solution and not part of the problem. Once you've chosen to approach a panicked diver too closely, you've exposed yourself to the possibility of loss of regulator and mask, dropped weight belt, and an exhausting struggle. Your approach to such a person needs to be *reasoned and practiced.*

Stay clear of a panicked person in the water until you're certain that you can either calm them down, or get control without undue risk to yourself. A panicky person in the water is seeking to get as high out of the water as possible and you may be just the stepping stone they need. Remember that, though this person may be a friend and long-time buddy, they are not rational. Their actions may place you in great danger as a result.

Panicky Diver Underwater

Panic underwater is most often triggered by breathing difficulties. The causes may range from over-exertion to actual out-of-air emergencies. Especially when working at depths, regulators may not always provide the diver with sufficient air for the activity level. Divers taking part in salvage operations, game collection, heavy exertion, or else simply over-weighted will sometimes work too hard, causing an apparent shortage of air. As inadequate ventilations continue, the diver's level of CO_2 in the blood stream rises, driving the diver to breathe faster. The sensation of air starvation can easily cause the diver to abandon all efforts to remain below and to bolt to the surface.

Divers unable to keep their buoyancy under control will also become increasingly frustrated and stressed. This might be caused by either over-weighting or under-weighting. Struggling to stay down or to stay off the bottom may cause anxiety and exertion in an improperly weighted diver. Novice divers in particular may frequently bounce up and down until they finally master the skill of good buoyancy control. This kind of activity could lead to ear and sinus pain, and an abrupt termination of the dive. A diver carrying a heavy bag of scallops or old bottles will struggle to near exhaustion without ever considering abandoning his booty. Frequently this diver gets into serious difficulty trying to remain on the surface. If on the surface, ask the diver to hand you the bag. Since you probably will be no better at keeping this load afloat, your best course of action will most likely be to drop the bag and mark it for later recovery.

Though a diver panicking underwater will most often try to escape to the surface as quickly as possible, sometimes he will act almost frozen with fear or behave erratically with rapid breathing and darting movements. This diver may reach unexpectedly for your regulator or his actions might dislodge your mask. Passive panic is not uncommon in aquatic emergencies, especially in those persons who have only limited watermanship skills to begin with. The feeling of general discomfort in the water combined with a sense of inability to help themselves in an aquatic crisis can cause some people to yield to their "fate" without a struggle. Their reaction can quickly shift, however, so exercise caution as you approach a breathing, but immobile person underwater.

Assisting Panicky Divers

Dive instruction trains our bodies and minds to deal effectively with the challenges associated with using dive equipment and dealing with the underwater environment. A diver in panic loses self-control and forgets the training that made him safe. This is why panic is so dangerous to the diver and to his buddy. A diver in this state makes no rational choices, only reacts to his fear, usually complicating the original situation that caused the panic in the first place.

Panicky diver in the water
• Stay clear until you assess the situation.
• Attempt to establish contact with the diver.
• Ask the diver to inflate his BC.
• If necessary, make the diver buoyant.
• Instruct the diver to take 2-3 full breaths.
• If warranted, tow the diver to safety.

Diver in Distress on the Surface

Assisting a panicky diver will hinge on our remaining part of the solution and not becoming part of the problem. This will mean, for a start, that we remain out of reach of the diver until we have decided on a course of action. On the surface a panicky diver reacts to anything within close proximity. The prudent course for the rescuer to follow is to keep at least 15 ft. away to avoid becoming a target of the diver's intentions. At this distance, the diver in distress may not even acknowledge the approach the rescuer. Attempt to establish contact with the diver by shouting or waving. If the diver responds, instruct him to inflate his buoyancy compensator and/or drop his weight belt. Watching the diver's response will give you a good clue to his mental state.

Often just establishing positive buoyancy will cause a diver to calm down. If the diver fails to respond to regain control, you may have to inflate the buoyancy compensator for him. This is best done from behind the diver, out of range of his grasp. You may be able to swim around him to do this, or you may need to submerge and then surface behind him.

Most any person in distress in the water will experience an alteration in breathing pattern. Typically this will be rapid, shallow breathing or panting. This is very inefficient as full ventilations are required to exchange gases effectively. As a result the diver will increase the feeling of suffocation and panic. This condition will rapidly result in exhaustion due to hypoxia (lowered blood level of oxygen) and the increasing sensation of air starvation due to the elevated level of the "breath trigger" gas, carbon dioxide.

To return the diver's blood gases to normal, many water rescue experts suggest that you should instruct the diver to lie back and take several deep breaths. This will very often transform a diver in distress into just a tired diver who could use some help in getting back to the boat or shore. During this tired diver tow, it is important to keep talking to the victim. Reassure him that you are helping and that you'll soon be back to safety. Encourage him to replace his mask and regulator if surface conditions are choppy. A wave in the face at this stage might start the panic syndrome all over again.

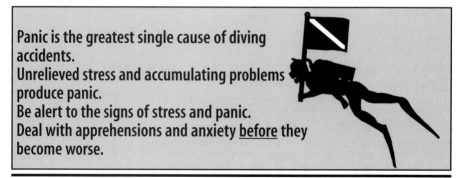

Panic is the greatest single cause of diving accidents.
Unrelieved stress and accumulating problems produce panic.
Be alert to the signs of stress and panic.
Deal with apprehensions and anxiety before they become worse.

Scuba I.Q. Review

1. What are some common sources of pre-dive stress?
2. How might you recognize stress in your dive buddy?
3. Describe some ways you might help reduce pre-dive stress in yourself and a buddy.
4. How can visualization be helpful to a scuba diver?
5. What factors may cause stress and panic in a diver while underwater?
6. What dangers does the rescuer face when attempting to help a panicky diver?
7. Why do alterations in breathing patterns affect a struggling or panicky diver?

Chapter 3
The Causes of Diving Accidents

How Diving Accidents Happen

In any recreation pursued as actively as scuba diving is, an occasional accident is inevitable. It is a tribute to recreational diver training standards, and instructors, that interested persons can usually be trained to adapt and operate so safely in an unforgiving environment. There is a persistent perception that scuba diving is highly dangerous, but it is less so than downhill skiing or even bicycling, both of which have higher accident rates. Most years more people in the US are killed by lightning strikes than by scuba diving accidents. In fact, scuba diving ranks below bowling in accident incident rating.

Exceeding prior experience and training

Ideally every dive will expand your underwater skills and knowledge so that you continue to pile up new techniques and solutions to problems. One way to provide yourself with growth opportunities is to find more experienced divers as potential dive buddies. Dive shops are a great place to find others who are looking for buddies. The shop itself may sponsor diving events that allow you to participate at your own level and still learn as you go. By participating in additional training with your instructor through your local dive store, you will get to know many other divers in your area.

Without participation from better trained and experienced divers, novices may well find themselves in difficulty if they undertake dives that surpass their ability. The first deep water dive, the first boat dive, the first night dive and many others may pose significant risks if proper planning and preparation doesn't precede these activities. Certain classes of dives, such as those deeper than 100 ft. (30 m), penetration wreck diving, cave diving and ice diving require specialized training before divers can engage in them properly. Ask your TDI/SDI instructor about advanced training available. You'll not only be safer, but find that diving is also a lot more enjoyable, too.

Accidents are often caused by divers exceeding their level of training. Operating in overhead environments calls for special preparation.

Cold or tired diver

A person in the water loses heat to the water many times faster than to air of the same temperature. Even in water at 80°F (26°C) a diver will eventually start to feel chilly after enough exposure. In fact the American Red Cross defines cold water as less than 70°F (21°C), a temperature that suggests that many of us dive in cold water year round. Wet suits are selected by thickness from 1 mm to 7 mm for the thermal protection they provide to divers in relatively warm to relatively cold waters. Below temperatures of about 55°F (13°C), however, many divers will choose to wear a dry suit, especially if they will be performing multiple dives. Nevertheless, any time we lose heat faster than we can produce it, we will eventually be affected by the cold. Apart from the effects of deep hypothermia which will be discussed later, the cold diver will experience a loss of energy and stamina.

Diving requires an output of energy, despite the peacefulness of the surroundings and the ease with which we glide through the water. Using the

Hypothermia is a factor in many diving accidents. Wear an exposure suit appropriate for the conditions and know your limits.

large muscles of the legs to propel ourselves through a thicker than normal medium, carrying and wearing heavy equipment, and sometimes having to swim against currents, we often expend more calories than we realize. Add to this an entry through surf or over rocks, climbing out of the water up a vertical ladder or hauling a camera and strobe or loaded game bag and the limits of our endurance may be reached before the dive is finished. A good level of physical fitness is a prerequisite to enjoyable diving; without it we may find ourselves unable to get to the exit point without assistance.

An alert observer or buddy will recognize the cold or tired diver by some similar characteristics. The diver will move slowly and often without following a consistent course. This diver will wander over the surface because he's too tired or cold to look where he's going. His movements may be uncoordinated and any operation such as inflating the BC may show the diver to have little control over his fine motor skills. Look also for frequent stops or rest breaks. The dive may even be motionless on the surface or underwater for long periods. Though not at a critical stage of hypothermia or exhaustion, any changes in sea state or weather may place this diver in immediate danger. Don't delay in offering appropriate assistance.

Muscle cramps

The physical fitness component may also make itself known during prolonged exercise when a diver develops muscle cramps. These are typically in

Long swims may cause muscle cramps. Contributing factors include cold water, dehydration, fins or fin straps too tight, or lack of physical conditioning.

the legs and most often in the calves and feet, though hamstring cramps are frequent as well. Prevention is always the best cure, so divers should strive to stay in good diving condition even in the "off season." A cramp, or forceful, continuous and involuntary muscle contraction, is caused by a muscle out-working its available blood supply. It may be brought on by sustained effort, poorly fitted fins, cold water, dehydration and inadequate nutrition. Cramps may be prevented by regular exercise, drinking plenty of clear fluids during the diving day, and wearing boots and fins that fit properly and keep you warm. Foods high in potassium such as bananas help the body maintain a good sodium to potassium ratio during exercise and will reduce the problem.

Overweighted diver

Many divers tend to forget that the reason they wear a weight belt or use an integrated weighting system is not to sink more easily, but to neutralize the buoyancy of their exposure suit. These divers, who may carry 5-10 lbs. more than they need, will rationalize their bad habit by stating that their BC will keep them afloat. The fact is, however, that we should never carry so much weight that we sink from the surface even with no air in the BC. Over-weighting is a dangerous practice and may lead to a diver's inability to remain on the surface in the event of unconsciousness or exhaustion. Over-weighting may be a significant contributing factor why the diver is in trouble to start with.

Good diving practice dictates that a diver should be neutrally buoyant at all times on a dive. On the surface we may choose to make ourselves more buoyant by adding air to the BC so that we'll stay higher above the surface. This can help keep our faces out of the waves and make it easier to talk to our buddy. Over-weighting makes it all the more difficult to do this and may even require that we fill the BC to capacity to stay afloat. This in turn will result in some difficulty swimming or reaching and handling other equipment. Ideally we are properly weighted when we exhale and sink slightly in the water. When we take a breath from the regulator, we should rise until our face is just above water level.

Over-weighting can sometimes be inadvertent as when a neutrally-buoyant salt water diver dives in freshwater or when new equipment is used for the first time or even if a different size tank is used. We need to remember that different circumstances may call for adjustments to our ballasting system.

Avoid accidents by:
• Staying within the limits of your training and experience.
• Keeping in good physical condition.
• Maintaining your equipment in good working order.
• Practicing neutral buoyancy.
• Getting sufficient rest before diving.

Pounding surf and rocky shorelines are a dangerous combination for divers.

Even on rough days there may be calmer water behind breakwaters and jetties.

Currents

Surface currents may pose a significant problem for divers in some areas. On the ocean we are affected by tides and wind-generated surface currents. While surge is mainly considered an underwater feature, its effect is still evident on the surface and may sweep a diver away from an exit point on the boat or shore.

Tides are predictable and generally well understood in local areas. A common misconception, however, is that tides simply come in and go out. After all, if we stand at the shore and watch the ocean, we see that the water level rises and falls over a period of time. We can easily believe that the water simply runs out and then comes back. The reality is that tides always have direction and close to shore that direction is almost always parallel to the shoreline. Divers planning their entries and exits need to take this into account to avoid a long, exhausting swim back against the current. Note current direction and speed by observing the way buoys or visible kelp lean with current and plan your route accordingly.

Surface currents where boat diving operations are planned may present an even greater problem for divers in the water. Currents may be too strong to swim against and sweep divers away from descent lines or from the boarding platform. The direction of any currents present can be easily determined by the direction in which the boat streams in the current when on anchor. Bear in mind, however, that small, flat-bottomed boats such as inflatables may be affected as much by the wind as by the current. A careful boat captain will trail a long, floating drift line aft of the boat to ensure that divers who are swept past the boat can haul themselves back against the current. Another prudent idea is to run a water-level line from the entry point to the descent line. Very often the descent line is the boat's anchor line off the front of the boat, and the entry point into the water is off the stern or side of the boat. A line between these two points (typically against the current) will allow divers to reach the descent line without a difficult swim before the dive starts.

Rips are another surface current that can cause difficulty to the diver. By definition they are relatively high speed currents that move out to sea from the shore. Rips may be produced by high tide waters accumulating behind barrier reefs and then flowing to seaward with great force as the tide changes. Many coral atolls are famous for their high water induced rips and present the diver with a localized, but powerful, out-bound current. In addition high tide waters may collect in small coves that also serve as the outlet of rivers. The combination of the falling tide outflow from the accumulated high tide water and the river flow may produce very significant currents that can easily overpower the diver.

In the marine environment, tides may set up longshore currents and rips. Rips can be identified by streams of foam set perpendicular to shore, while longshore currents show themselves as irregular lines of foam running parallel to shore.

Rips may also be produced by currents that move parallel to the shoreline. Tides are the most frequent causes of "longshore currents," though they may also be caused by persistent wind and wave action moving together in the same direction. When these longshores meet an underwater obstruction, a portion of the water is diverted directly out to sea, producing a rip. Almost any beach will demonstrate such rips that come and go with tidal flow.

A good guide to the presence and location of rips and longshores is the presence of foam or discolored water moving in straggly lines across the surface of the water. Rips will run into and be collected by longshores. A diver's pre-dive scene survey should include looking for and noting the location of these currents. In particular the diver's route should consider planning an exit away from rips, though the entry may be in a rip to speed the diver outbound, especially when entering in surf. A rescue diver might also use the power of a rip to speed him to the scene.

Escaping from rips and longshore currents usually requires the same method, i.e., swimming perpendicular to the current. Both rips and longshores are normally narrow flows and are soon left behind. The important thing is not to panic, to swim at a comfortable pace and plan exactly where

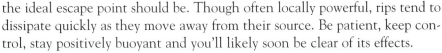

Ocean Currents
• Tides, rips, and longshore currents can be overpowering if you try to swim against them.
• Start your dive against the current when you're fresh, warm, and have plenty of air. Use the current to help you back.
• Learn to pick out evidence of surface currents before you dive so that you can accommodate them into your dive plan.

the ideal escape point should be. Though often locally powerful, rips tend to dissipate quickly as they move away from their source. Be patient, keep control, stay positively buoyant and you'll likely soon be clear of its effects.

In any case vigilance on the part of divers in the water and observers onboard dive vessels or on shore is essential to notice early stages of a diver having difficulties. Currents are relentless and unforgiving while the diver's stamina is limited. Rapid and appropriate intervention will save a situation from evolving into an exhausted-diver rescue.

In areas of strong surface currents, the dive boat should have a drift line floating down current for divers to hold onto while waiting their turn to board the boat.

Freshwater diving

Freshwater is also often characterized by the presence of currents. In general the current velocities in moving freshwater far exceed those in the ocean. Diving activities in rivers and streams must take into account the forces that act on the diver's body due to drag, and these forces may be considerable. An ocean rip or tidal flow may move faster than a diver can swim, but river speeds may push and tumble a diver out of control. In addition an ocean diver will probably not encounter the kinds of underwater obstructions that the river diver will face.

Fallen trees, numerous abandoned monofilament fishing lines, and bridge pilings are just a few of the underwater hazards in rivers. A diver snagged in the branches of a submerged tree faces a life-threatening emergency. Current velocities of only 5 knots (1 knot = about 100ft./min. or about 6 miles per hour) will exert a force of more than 575 lbs. on an upright diver and nearly 100 lbs. on a horizontal diver. River flow can easily exceed 2 or 3 times this speed, making a diver tangled in an underwater obstruction in dire circumstances, indeed. With a force a thousand pounds or more pressing the diver farther into the entanglement, his chances of self-rescue are remote. Divers should *never* enter water moving at speeds greater than just a few knots unless they have been specially trained for such environments.

Freshwater diving is often characterized by strong currents. Directly downstream of an emerged object there will always be a current reversal, an eddy that moves upstream.

Diving in fast moving rivers is extremely hazardous.
• Flowing water is enormously powerful and can easily sweep a diver away.
• Underwater entanglements may pose greater safety risks in rivers than in still water.
• Be especially wary of eddies, hydraulics, and strainers.
• Anything that interrupts the main direction of a river current will result in current reversals that can trap a diver underwater. Learn to read the river.

Other currents operate in rivers, as well. Whenever an obstruction emerges from moving water, a predictable eddy or current reversal will form downstream of the object. This eddy moves exactly in the opposite direction of the main flow of the stream. Current reversals are typically found below (downstream) bridge pilings, emerged rocks and outcrops that protrude into the current. Since these reversals are predictable from the observable topography, divers and boaters can take advantage of them to exit from the main current either in mid-stream or along the shoreline. Divers in distress on the surface will frequently be carried into eddies where they can be reached and assisted.

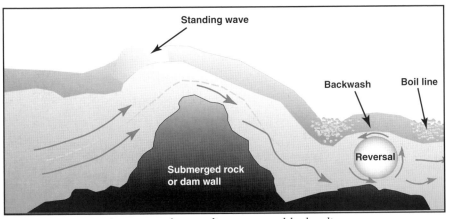

Anatomy of a standing wave and hydraulic.

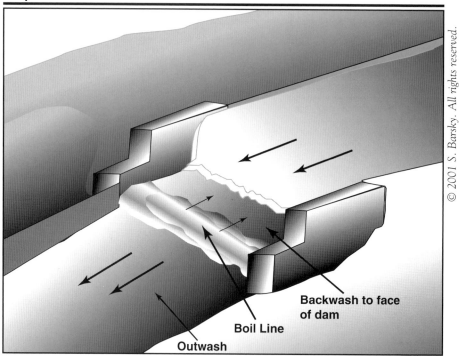

**Backwash to face
of dam**

Boil Line

Outwash

Water flow over a low-head dam.

*Powerful hydraulics are formed in moving water. The circular motion when water
drops even a few feet can pin a person to the bottom.*

Objects that do not emerge above the surface of the water may produce treacherous reversals called hydraulics. Hydraulics are actually vertical eddies that constantly recirculate below (downstream) the submerged object. The danger is that a diver may be carried to and pinned on the bottom by the relentless current. In strong currents escape may be very difficult, though the diver has a much better chance of escape than a pinned swimmer or boater. Most persons who are drowned in hydraulics are pinned long enough to run out of breath. A diver has the advantage of an air supply, exposure suit and buoyancy compensator. The recommended method of escape is to swim on the bottom as deep as possible to emerge downstream. If the obstruction causing the hydraulic is only a rock or small shelf, it may be best to swim out to the side to escape the direct effects of the hydraulic. Surfacing too soon may result in being carried back upstream by the reversing current and pulled underwater again, a cycle that may be repeated several times.

A special example of a hydraulic is a low-head dam. This is a truly dangerous aspect of river diving. In a low-head dam flood waters are held back by a low wall that simply allows high water to over-flow and be carried downstream. Typically these passive water control dams have no release gates that can be closed to remove a trapped person. A person trapped, therefore, is caught in a hydraulic that extends across the entire river, making escape to the sides more difficult. An underwater swim on the bottom is probably the only realistic method of escaping these killer currents.

Gear problems

Well maintained diving equipment rarely fails during a dive. Since this equipment is manufactured for life-support and the diver's life and well-being depend on it, it is only reasonable that a thinking diver will look after it. Annual service for regulators and buoyancy compensators, as well as certified inspection for scuba cylinders, is one good way to guarantee that the equipment will perform as required when it's really needed.

Regulators will usually malfunction in one of two ways. Most likely is that a regulator will "free-flow," i.e., deliver air flow continuously even though the diver is not attempting to inhale. Sometimes this caused by a deviation in the intermediate pressure being released by the first stage, which in turn forces the second stage to open and allow the air out. In other instances we associate a free-flow with the growth of ice in either the first or second stage valve mechanisms. The water need not be freezing cold for this to happen; a deep dive with its associated high air demands and thus cooling effect of air passing through valve stems, may be sufficient to cause ice to form. Water temperatures of less than 50°F (10°C) will be cool enough to bring about this effect.

In either case a free-flowing regulator is not necessarily an immediate crisis. It's certainly possible to breathe from a free-flowing regulator, though the diver must be careful not to seal the lips completely around the mouthpiece. The trick is to permit sufficient air to escape so that the lungs do not over-inflate. This is not at all difficult, though the diver would be wise to practice this technique by simulating a free-flow by gently pushing the purge button on the second stage. A note of caution; a full-blown free-flow may well propel the second stage out of the diver's mouth. Also, a slow free-flow often progresses into a full free-flow with a resulting rapid lose of air. With this in mind it would be sensible to terminate the dive when a free-flow begins.

Another type of regulator malfunction is a "freeze up." Again a phenomenon generally associated with cold water, a freeze up occurs when water in the air supply forms a chip of ice in the air passage of the first stage and thus blocks further air flow. The source of this water may be from the scuba cylinder itself, if filled from an inadequately maintained compressor. TDI/SDI recommends that divers take their tanks for fills only to certified fill stations. This is the best way to ensure that the air is dry and contaminant free.

Water may also enter the first stage if the dust cap is not replaced after every dive, or during the post-dive washing/rinsing process. This serves to highlight the importance of drying the dust cap before replacing it after a dive. No water should ever be permitted to enter the exposed portion of the air intake on the regulator's first stage. For the same reason, the purge button of the second stage should never be pressed while it is underwater and not pressurized from the tank. Water may seep into the second stage and find its way up the hose to the first stage. This may result in a freeze up or free-flow, due to icing, when the regulator is next used.

Given enough time and use, nearly every device will fail. This also holds true for regulator hoses. Hose protectors are the best way to ensure that constant flexing and handling will not prematurely deteriorate the hoses, but eventually any hose can fail and rupture. On the surface a hose may fail with an explosive bang and hiss of escaping air that will startle anyone standing nearby. Though no real damage to other parts or injuries to persons are likely to result from this, the dive obviously cannot go ahead until the hose is replaced.

Hose failure underwater also occurs. The sound is dampened, of course, but still obvious, and the constant hiss of bubbles confirms what has just happened. High pressure hose breaks are usually quite loud, even underwater, but the amount of air lost is both constant and relatively small. A low pressure hose break will dump air much more quickly due to larger hose diameter and the fact that the first stage will deliver air at a higher rate in deeper water. Several hundred pounds of air pressure may be lost before the diver reaches the surface. For this reason any hose break spells the immediate end to the dive. This is also part of the reason that the 500 p.s.i. end pressure rule was originally developed. The practice of "running on empty" or completely depleting the tank contents puts the diver at risk of catastrophic air loss if a hose breaks or a free-flow occurs.

Other gear problems may occur during a dive. A broken mask strap or fin strap may cause the loss of these items. Most often, however, the diver will complete the entire dive without even knowing that a strap is broken. Water pressure often keeps the mask in place and suction in the foot pocket of the fin keeps it on without benefit of straps. Still, these items may be lost or dislodged underwater, and the prepared diver will know how to adapt.

Our eyes can only see clearly when there is an air space in front of them. This is the reason we need the mask in the first place, to preserve the air space. Looking for a dropped or dislodged mask on the bottom can be difficult since our eyes will not be able to distinguish the mask from the background clearly. We can simulate a mask by creating a temporary air space that may give us enough time to locate our mask. Cup your hands around your eyes and collect bubbles of exhaled breath in these pockets. Air will leak from the pockets you've created, but you may have time to see where the dropped mask is and retrieve it. Remember to keep your head down to help hold in the trapped air.

If a fin is lost underwater, you may be able to find it if you know where to look. The older style black rubber fins will always sink to the bottom, while thermoplastic fins will normally rise to the surface. It's a good idea to test your fins to find out how they will act both in freshwater, where they may be in mid-water, and in salt water, where they float at the surface. If the fin cannot be found, consider using the dolphin kick while swimming. The foot without the fin can be locked behind the foot with the fin and both legs can be used to propel you. You can get a surprisingly powerful kick using both legs and only one fin. To ease the recovery of a lost fin, some divers attach brightly colored tabs to the straps. The tabs are used to help pull the straps on and off the boot, but also serve as great visual aids in locating a lost fin.

Injuries

Divers may be injured on the surface by means that really have nothing to do with diving. For example, we typically dive around boats and are therefore always at some risk of being threatened or even struck by a passing boat. In fact, it's not a rare occurrence for a diver to be run over by his own tending boat. From the point of view of our own safety we seek to minimize this danger through the use of dive flags.

Ultimately, panic or the loss of self-control, is the most common factor in diving accidents.

The most widely recognized flag is the red and white Diver Down flag. Ideally this should be flown directly over the submerged divers. To provide an even greater level of safety divers should seriously consider towing a buoy with the Diver Down flag displayed.

A second flag that indicates the presence of divers is flag "Alpha." This flag gets its name from the fact that it is the letter "A" in the flag alphabet. Technically, this flag should be flown on the dive boat as it specifically indicates a vessel which is unable to maneuver due to the presence of divers below. As such it is commonly seen being flown from a vessel that has divers below who may actually be working on an underwater job, either on the bottom or perhaps even making repairs to the vessel itself. For this reason it is often referred to as the "commercial diver's flag," though this is misleading. If the dive boat is at anchor and there are divers in the water, it would be appropriate to warn other boaters to the fact of divers in the water. The divers themselves should tow the Diver Down flag to indicate their exact position.

The use of the Alpha flag bestows specific rights of location to the dive scene. The Alpha flag is a warning to boat operators that means, "I have a diver down. Keep well clear and at slow speed." Conversely, regulations regarding the sport diving flag vary from state to state, and sometimes from county to county. Be sure to check local regulations in your area.

Keep in mind that diving in marked or accustomed ship channels will call for special permission from local authorities. In addition, other local "off limits" areas may be closed to divers.

Despite these precautions, accidents do happen. Divers on the surface may be very seriously injured, even killed, by boats. Head injuries are a typical result though broken arms, collar bones and neck injuries are frequent, as well. Head wounds may bleed profusely and neck injuries may result in severe

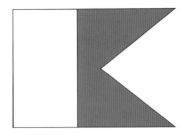

The Alpha flag is used to indicate that a vessel is restricted in its ability to maneuver because it has divers in the water.

compromise to motor skills, feeling and even the ability to breathe. Handling a head or neck injured person requires great skill and practice. *Always* call for professional assistance in these cases.

A propeller injury from a boat that passes completely over a diver on the surface may be a horrific sight. Prevention of blood loss and subsequent shock, treating open wounds, and dealing with the expected head and neck injuries make the first responder a potential life saver. Training in first aid and the presence of a good first aid kit will be necessary to keep the patient alive long enough to reach definitive emergency care. Are you ready?

Other non-diving hazards that the diver will face is the sometimes rocky shoreline from which so many of our best dives start. Wearing or carrying nearly a hundred pounds of equipment over jagged or slippery rocks is an invitation to leg and ankle injuries. Most of these accidents will take place before the diver even enters the water. Still, they are dive site injuries and we need to be prepared for the eventuality. Again, first aid training that includes on-scene treatment for sprains, bruises, scrapes and cuts will make the dive rescue specialist an invaluable part of the dive team. Have a first aid kit that includes cold packs for bumps and sprains, heat packs for cold fingers and toes, small to large Band-Aids, absorbent dressings and tape for larger cuts and scrapes, elastic wraps, sterile water, tweezers, shears or scissors, seasickness pills, sunblock and burn cream, and a first aid manual. For a complete inventory of a rescue diver's first aid kit, see the Appendix.

Most dive site injuries are minor and have little to do with actual diving. Be prepared to deal with strains, sprains, cuts, and scrapes.

Hyperthermia

A somewhat unexpected environmental injury is hyperthermia or elevated body core temperature. We may probably be more used to the idea of a *drop* in the body core temperature while diving, so that over-heating tends to get over-looked. Divers in full wet suits or in dry suits, however, may be at risk in warm conditions if there is delay in getting into the water or if they exert themselves carrying gear to the dive site.

Normally, our bodies produce more heat than we actually need, so we have several mechanisms for getting rid of excess heat. Perspiring and losing heat through evaporation is a familiar method for dumping heat. We may even douse ourselves with water to hasten the process. We also lose heat by warming the air in contact with the skin. This process is called "conduction" and is the same method we use to warm the water in our wet suits. Fanning ourselves or standing in a breeze removes the warmed air from around our skin and from inside our clothes by a process called "convection." Lastly, we emit infrared "radiation" which also results in a heat loss. Note that all these methods take place on the skin. Once we put on a wet or dry suit, we are effectively cut off from the outside and can no longer transmit surplus heat to the environment. That is, of course, the whole point of the exposure suit.

Hypothermia

The effects of cold-water immersion are insidious, creeping up on us, sometimes unnoticed until the diver suddenly feels cold. The diver's exposure suit traps heat for varying lengths of time depending on the water temperature, and type and thickness of the suit. As our body core temperature drops with prolonged exposure, we begin to undergo physiological changes that diminish our senses of awareness and survival skills. We fight the effects of heat loss in two ways, by increasing heat production and by decreasing heat loss.

We produce heat through normal metabolic processes and through direct muscular activity. If our present level of activity is insufficient to maintain a body core temperature of at least $97^{0}F$ ($36^{0}C$), we start to shiver. Shivering is actually an exceptionally effective method of producing heat and, from the point of view of the rescuers, always a good sign since it indicates a body that is still fighting heat loss. As the body continues to cool, shivering may become much more vigorous, even violent, as the body becomes desperate to keep the core and brain warm. The brain also directs the body to take action to conserve heat as much as possible. The vast majority of heat is lost through the skin via the mechanisms outlined earlier. This heat is transported to the skin by the circulation which carries it up from the core. To prevent this heat loss, the brain constricts the blood vessels under the skin and instead directs the circulation to shunt the blood between itself, the lungs and the major organs only. The skin and extremities are allowed to cool as the brain attempts to conserve heat and, thus, life.

Divers facing uncontrolled heat loss will eventually lose their ability to think rationally and to function normally. This is an exceedingly dangerous situation for a diver who may need to make a number of survival choices, most of which will require good motor skills. Fingers become so numbed that weight belts cannot be dropped, masks remain uncleared and all thoughts of the buddy system disappear.

All divers must remain alert to the challenges imposed by temperature considerations. Frequent buddy checks need to be completed to ensure that all divers are comfortable during the dive. Knowing that a typical agreement between divers is that when one diver is cold and wants to go back that all will go back puts the cold diver in the position of "ruining" everyone's dive. We all need to be sensitive to the exposure that each of us faces, and conduct the dive accordingly. Never expose your buddy or any other member of the dive group to hazards or circumstances for which they are unprepared.

Almost all dive accidents are preventable. Decide what you're going to do before you do it. Pay attention to what you're doing and stay alert.

Case histories

Understanding the most frequent causes of diving accidents, and reading first-hand accounts and reconstruction of investigated accidents, often leaves the rescue diver breathless with the degree of misfortune (and, sometimes, stupidity) that befalls their fellow divers. Below is a brief selection of accident descriptions, chosen from many, that highlight how and why things go wrong underwater.

Case 1

A group of people in two boats traveled out onto the lake amid storm warnings, and two divers entered the water for the purpose of inspecting a submerged fishing net on the bottom of the lake. Visibility was approximately 10 ft. (3 m) and the divers quickly became separated. The first diver surfaced, waited a couple of minutes and dived again to look for his buddy. The buddy surfaced looking for the first diver, waited a couple of minutes and then dived to look for him. The first diver surfaced again, looked around and immediately dived again.

The first diver found his buddy tangled in the fishing net on the bottom, snagged by the tank valve and struggling to get free. The first diver tried to cut his buddy out of the net, but ran out of air. He swam to the boat through 7 ft. (2 m) seas and had the remaining people on board call the Coast Guard. The Coast Guard responded, but had no diver. A Sheriff's department diver later recovered the buddy, still tangled in the net.

Analysis:
1. A severe weather warning was in effect.
2. The first diver had about 100 logged dives; the second diver was uncertified and had done only one prior dive.
3. The victim was using borrowed equipment and had no knife.
4. As determined in the autopsy, the victim's blood alcohol level was twice the legal limit.
5. No dive plan, emergency procedures or contingency plans were discussed.

Case 2

Three divers arrived at a frozen lake to try their hands at ice diving. None of the three had any experience at ice diving, but the "senior" diver present was a certified Divemaster and had talked to other ice divers about the techniques involved. A hole was cut in the ice just large enough for a single diver to enter at a time. This meant that the first diver in had to submerge to allow

Ice diving is a specialized activity requiring careful planning, plenty of topside support, and trained divers.

the second diver to enter. The first diver in had a tending line attached to her BC with a locking carabiner and was connected to the second diver by a buddy line which they held between them. The Divemaster tended the divers and also was to serve as the rescue diver in the event of a problem.

After about three minutes into the dive, the tending line went slack and the Divemaster realized that the divers were off the line. He donned his equipment and, holding a line 50% longer than used by the women and tied off on a stake driven into the ice, started a search for the missing divers. He swam a complete circle around the hole, hoping to snag the divers, but without success. He then did a bottom search at the extent of his line, again without success. During this search he discovered that part of the area they were diving had depths in excess of 90 ft. (27 m), though they believed the maximum depth in the area to be 30 ft. (9 m). He also made numerous ascents to the underside of the ice and back down again from the deepest part of the dive. He reasoned that he might still have missed the divers if they were just under the ice and so tried to look everywhere at once.

The Divemaster eventually returned to the hole out of air and frantic. He summoned help, but local police divers were unable to locate the missing divers. Their bodies were recovered in the spring nearly a quarter of a mile away from the hole. When found, both tanks were empty and both women still had their weight belts on. The Divemaster showed signs and symptoms of DCS and was recompressed at a local facility.

Analysis

1. Divers all exceeded their prior training and experience in a very high risk situation. Diving under overhead environments requires specialized, certified training. It is not sufficient to read about it in a book. The dive group made many unforgivable errors in procedure.

2. By definition, a dive tender cannot be the rescue diver. Rescue divers must be fully-geared up and ready to enter the water in seconds.

3. The rescue divers must be specially trained for these kinds of high-risk diving applications.

4. The critical line signals used to communicate between the tender and divers were made up on the spot. After the fact, the Divemaster could not even remember what they were.

5. We will never know exactly why the divers became lost, but speculation must account for the tethered diver deliberately disconnecting herself from the line. Possibly they dropped the handheld line and the second diver separated from the first. The first diver may have swum after her buddy and felt she had to release herself from the line to catch her. Once the connection back to the hole is broken, it is virtually impossible to find the hole again. The fact that the divers were found so far from the entry point suggests that they, indeed, swam a long way looking for a way out.

Scuba I.Q. Review

1. List four common problems that may lead to diving accidents.
2. Relative to the observer on the shore, in which direction do the tides run?
3. What is one way of solving the problem of divers being unable to swim back to the dive boat against the current?
4. What are rip currents? How are they formed?
5. Describe the danger of strainers to river divers.
6. Why are low-head dams and other hydraulics so dangerous to divers?
7. The water need not be freezing cold for a free-flow or freeze up to occur. Why is this so?
8. What kinds of injuries might you expect to find on a diver struck by a boat?

9. List four ways in which our bodies lose heat to the environment.

10. Describe the two main methods the body uses to manage heat loss in cold water.

11. Discuss the dangers of diving in overhead environments without specialized training.

Chapter 4
Responding to Emergencies on the Surface

Recognition

Ultimately all scuba diving rescues and assists become surface rescues. Indeed, most accidents happen at or near the surface, even if the situation began to develop underwater. Our principle role as a rescuer in a true underwater emergency will likely be to get the victim to the surface as quickly as possible in most cases. It's only on the surface that we can really give the kind of assistance required for most serious diving injuries. There are exceptions to this, as will be discussed in Chapter 5.

The kind of help we can provide to a buddy may take a large variety of forms, depending on the nature of the problem. In this chapter we will look at surface assists, towing of unconscious divers, in-water rescue breathing and methods to remove a helpless person from the water to the shore or dive boat. First, however, we have to able to recognize a diver in trouble.

Staying alert to trouble

Despite the relaxing nature of scuba diving, we will always be better prepared for an in-water or underwater emergency if we anticipate problems. Not only do we need to have ready skills, but we also need to pay attention to our buddy and to what's going on around us. Divers frequently become so inwardly focused as they cruise through their surroundings that they miss important clues to trouble elsewhere. Keep your ears open for the sound of approaching watercraft overhead, banging on a tank, a whistle or shout in the distance. Keep your eyes open for the signs of a diver in distress or showing discomfort.

1. Encountering or observing a diver alone, whether on the surface or underwater, could suggest that buddies are separated or that one surfaced in haste.

2. Divers observed in unlikely areas such as breaking surf zone, amid fishing or lobster trap buoys, in ship channels or over deep water without obvious surface support may be divers in trouble.

3. Watch a diver's bubbles. Prolonged intervals between breaths may indicate skip-breathing or a continuous stream may indicate a free-flowing regulator. Learn the difference between the appearance of bubbles when a diver is surfacing from when he is swimming or stationary. A diver surfacing produces a nearly continuous stream of bubbles that appear to "spread" over the surface. Note that these bubbles are not truly continuous as in a free-flow, but actually arrive at the surface in bursts. A diver that appears to be surfacing, then swimming horizontally, then surfacing again and again may be experiencing buoyancy or equalization problems.

4. Look closely at a diver who is very high in the water or very low in the water. The first may have dropped the weight belt due to some emergency and the second may be seriously over-weighted. The "heavy" diver may disappear off the surface just by raising the arm to wave for help.

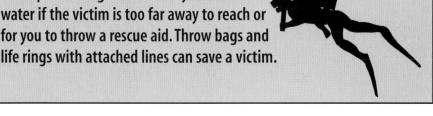

Whenever possible, stay out of the water when performing a rescue. Only enter the water if the victim is too far away to reach or for you to throw a rescue aid. Throw bags and life rings with attached lines can save a victim.

Response options

Reach or throw

In any rescue situation we need always to remember that our own safety comes first. Though highly motivated and perhaps even personally involved with the diver in distress, we may accomplish nothing if we ignore the risk to ourselves in our response. In a few incautious moments the situation may end up with one more victim and one less rescuer. If the person is within reach of the shore or boat, you may be able to stretch your arm out to help the person to the boat or wharf.

To avoid being pulled in yourself, stay as low as possible and keep as much of your weight away from the edge as you can. Not only is this safer, but it also allows you a longer reach. Use an oar, boat hook, branch or even jumper cables to extend your reach. If the victim is out of reach, the best action is often simply to throw a rescue device to the person needing help. Examples of throwable devices include life rings, throw bags and a personal flotation device (PFD). Once the person in distress grasps the device, it is a simple matter of pulling him back to the boat or shore. This keeps us from having to enter the water and is actually a speedier response.

Having or throwing a flotation device in the water gives an exhausted diver a place to rest on the surface.

Stay low and keep your center of gravity away from the edge when reaching out to a person in the water.

Poor lifting technique! Keep your legs bent and weight low when lifting someone onto a wharf or into a boat.

Use a throwable device with a line attached to it to pull a struggling person back to safety.

Swimming rescues

In situations where we cannot reach victims from shore or the boat, we may have to enter the water to assist them. Do not undertake long swims unless you are certain of your ability to cover the distance and return towing a helpless person. This may well be much more difficult than you think unless these are practiced skills. The TDI/SDI Rescue Diver course will help develop the skills you'll need to do this effectively. The rescue can be made easier and safer if you remember to take a flotation device with you. Hand the victim the rescue device while you retain your grip on it. Use it to tow the victim back. This provides the victim with additional flotation and keeps him at least arm's length away. This may be important if the victim is panicky or might become so.

The best swimming approach to a person on the surface is the head-up front crawl. This allows us to observe the victim continually as we come closer in the event they disappear off the surface. Stop and observe the behavior of the victim from about 15 ft. (5 m) away before coming any closer. If the victim seems under control, then close the distance and extend the buoyancy device to him. Instruct the victim to roll over on his back and to take several deep breaths. Most persons in trouble in the water will become short of breath and start to feel as if they are suffocating. Re-establishing a positive blood gas balance will go a long way to calming a distressed person.

A panicky diver is a significant danger to himself and everyone around him.

A swimmer who is dispatched to assist a diver on the surface can be pulled back, together with the victim, by using an attached tether line.

The rescuer must possess good self-control and swimming skills to attempt a rescue in surf and near emerged rocks.

Make it a point to talk to the victim as you continue the tow. Panicky or distressed persons in the water are usually their own worst enemies. Talking to them continually and reassuring them that you'll soon be back to safety will greatly assist their ability to regain self-control. Take care not to exert yourself unduly; we may finish up with two victims and no rescuers. It will be a major asset to you if you have attached a tether line to yourself before beginning the swim. This way both of you can be pulled to safety without the effort of towing a passive person. This also leaves your hands free to deal with the victim more effectively.

Panicky diver on the surface

A panicky diver represents a considerable threat to himself and to all others around him. The unreasoning fear that grips an out-of-control person is self-perpetuating and may even be contagious. Being dragged down by being over-weighted or over-burdened, not being able to breathe due to a too tight wet suit, a too tight dry suit neck seal, a poorly maintained regulator, feeling defenseless in slapping waves or strong currents all can produce the surging fear that results in panic. Panic is the loss of self-control. A diver in panic forgets the things he needs to know and do to take care of himself.

Dive training is essentially constructed so as to condition our minds and bodies to the fact that we are perfectly capable of breathing and staying underwater for long periods of time. After all, this is not a natural act, and we must *learn* to be comfortable while scuba diving. It is our self-control and understanding through experience that allows us to relax underwater. The diver, stressed by circumstance and vulnerable to the environment, may panic.

A diver on the surface who is clearly in distress and struggling needs assistance immediately. The longer the diver is overpowered by panic, the greater is the danger of exhaustion and possible drowning. Still, the responding rescuer must exercise caution in an approach to a panicky diver. You should stop while you are still out of reach and try to communicate with the victim. Sometimes the nearby presence of another diver, calm and in control, will be reassurance enough to relieve his sense of isolation. Often, however, the panicky diver is so withdrawn and detached from rationality that he won't respond to you at a distance.

If you decide that you must physically help the diver, you would be prudent to inflate your BC slightly first before approaching too closely. In case the diver grasps you, you need to have enough buoyancy to prevent being pulled underwater by a sinking victim. The possibility of having to retrieve a sinking victim is very real, and a good argument for keeping your weight belt

Waste no time in responding to a person in distress in the water.

on unless there is a compelling reason to drop it. The most important immediate assistance you can provide, therefore, is to make the diver fully buoyant. If your shouted instructions to inflate his BC are ignored or the diver is unable to do this himself, you'll need to do it for him. Carefully circle around behind him and reach over his shoulder for the inflator hose. Keep your other hand on his tank valve so that he can't easily turn around and intercept you. A panicky diver will likely see you as a "stepping stone" to get himself higher out of the water. Keep him at arm's length until you've inflated the BC.

In many instances this will be enough in itself to calm a panicky diver. In choppy conditions, however, and where the diver has discarded his mask and regulator, he is still at considerable risk of inhaling water and being blinded by spray. Assist the diver in recovering his regulator and turning him

A panicky diver needs assistance, but the rescuer must be mindful of his own safety. Keep your distance until you can get control.

away from the waves. If the diver remains out of control, you may need to tow him directly back to the dive boat or shore. Talk to the diver continually and reassure him that you both soon be in a safe place. He'll calm down eventually as he realizes that he's no longer in danger of sinking and that help is at hand.

You may not be able to approach too closely to a panicked diver without making yourself a target of his attentions. If he reaches for you and you're within range, you will likely be in for a struggle and end up losing your own mask and regulator. Your best course of action is to fall back into the defensive position. Swim away on your back while keeping your eyes on the victim. Underwater and out of sight of the victim, bring one knee close to surface and extend your fin toward him. If the diver gets too close, plant your foot on his chest and *gently* push yourself away from him. In your haste to keep your distance, don't become alarmed yourself and kick the victim. This could easily cause a serious chest trauma. Also, be very careful of the position of your fin tips. They may be close to the victim's throat and can cause him considerable injury. Thermoplastic fins, in particular, can be worn down to rough, sharp edges. Swim in the direction of safety; the diver may follow you there!

If you're within range of the victim's reach and too close to adopt the defensive posture, you may have to get immediate control of a panicky diver. You may choose to do this anyway if delaying assistance leaves the victim in

To establish control immediately, or if you can't get out of the way quickly enough, grasp the victim's hand or wrist as they reach for you to gain control.

Pull hard to spin the victim around and then quickly inflate their BC.

Once they are fully buoyant, most people will calm down.

rocks in rough seas. As the diver reaches out to you, you'll respond by grasping his wrist with your opposite hand. Pull the victim toward you *hard*. This will cause both of you to spin and leave you directly behind the diver. Immediately reach over his shoulder for the inflator, make him buoyant and begin the tow to safety.

Panic may overtake a diver without warning. In the same way you may be surprised by the panicky diver in close proximity who suddenly has you in a death grip. Even a relatively small person can exert incredible force when driven by panic, and can overpower the unwary buddy. This is a very dangerous position for the rescuer who will likely lose mask, regulator and buoyancy as the panicked diver tries to climb up higher out of the water. At this stage you are both victims. Your best avenue of escape will usually be to sink underwater. The last place the panicked diver wants to go is down, so pursuit there is unlikely. Dragging the victim down with you will usually result in your rapid release. If you are unable to let air out of your BC and sink, you'll need to break free of the victim's grip first.

As the diver's arm encircles your head or neck, turn your face away from the crook of his arm and toward his hand. Grasp his elbow with the hand nearest the crook of his arm while grasping his hand or wrist with your other hand. Push up on his elbow and pull out on his hand. This results in your sinking and his arm twisting away from you. Immediately get clear of the victim and prepare to get control of the situation. This escape will work on both front and back assaults from panicky divers and swimmers.

These defenses, escapes and control moves are valuable assets for any diver to possess. They are especially important for rescue divers to master. In common with all specialized skills, practice and repetition are essential to make them second nature. Always remember, however, that your own safety is your primary responsibility. Be cautious and stay within your level of training and capability when responding to panicky persons in the water. You'll always be safer and usually more effective if you take a flotation aid with you.

Tired diver assist

The physical demands of scuba diving are rarely more manifest than when a fully equipped diver has to swim on the surface. The weight belt seems to sag down around your ankles, the BC always seems to be in your face and you can't use your snorkel as easily. If it's choppy, you'll switch to your regulator, but that doesn't work as effectively in the air as it does underwater. Especially swimming back after a dive, the diver is likely to be tired and possibly chilled to start with; a long swim to shore may just be too much. It's no wonder that the most common rescue is the tired diver assist.

It's worth pointing out that a long surface swim is usually the result of poor planning. A good plan will lay out a route that returns the divers as close as possible to the exit point. A poor plan will not take into account any existing currents and their direction, surface conditions and prevailing winds. An additional common feature of the swim, besides environmental conditions, is that divers tend to become inwardly focused as they labor toward their goal. The consequence is that the divers often become separated on the surface. It becomes less apparent, then, when one begins to lag behind due to tiredness or muscle cramps. Frequent buddy checks will prevent separation at the surface, as well as save a search and the anxious moments that go along with it.

When you notice your buddy or another diver lagging well behind the rest of the group, you should make an effort to establish contact. It can be frightening for a less fit diver to be left behind, especially if already tired. Early intervention can be crucial in preventing a tired diver from becoming a panicky diver. Talk calmly to the tired diver while you determine whether there are any other associated or potential problems such as muscle cramps, overweighting, low air supply, too much or too little buoyancy, cold, etc. It may be necessary to assist the diver in the swim back by towing him. To do this, ask the diver to stay on his back while you hold him by the tank valve. Make yourself suitably buoyant and pull him with you. Most often the tired diver will be able to contribute some finning to the effort after a few moments rest. In any case take the tow in good time so as to avoid over-exerting yourself. If the diver is not your buddy, be sure to let your buddy know when you go to assist someone else. He may be organizing a search to look for you!

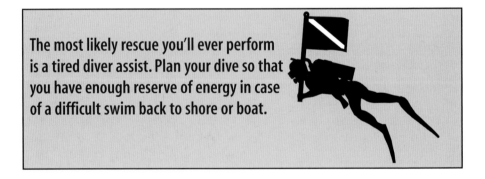

The most likely rescue you'll ever perform is a tired diver assist. Plan your dive so that you have enough reserve of energy in case of a difficult swim back to shore or boat.

A common rescue is the tired diver assist. Reassure your buddy that you can help him, have him become positively buoyant and tow him from the tank valve or BC. If conditions are choppy, ask him to keep his mask on.

It is easier and safer to tow your buddy if he can hold onto a flotation aid.

Diver in distress on the surface

Most diving accidents happen at or near the surface. A solo diver on the surface may be simply orienting himself, resting or may have been the victim of a diving accident. Until you get closer to the diver, you may have no idea whether the diver is having an actual problem. Certainly, it's always appropriate to give the "OK" signal to a diver on the surface to assure yourself that the diver does not need assistance. Lack of a reply can be taken as an indication that the diver does, indeed, have a problem. He may, in fact, be unable to answer.

Conscious Diver

A conscious diver will acknowledge your approach, which, as always, should be slow and circumspect. Visual clues will help you sort through possibilities to assess the situation. What drew your attention in the first place? Was the diver struggling? listless? floating on his back? As you approach, note whether the mask is on, the regulator in his mouth and air is in the BC. This might indicate that he ditched them in panic or a struggle underwater. Is he exceptionally high in the water? This might indicate a dropped weight belt and fully inflated BC which might in turn suggest a too rapid ascent from depth.

Ask the diver to tell you his air pressure. The amount of air left may also imply an out-of-air emergency and his actions may hint at lung injuries or decompression sickness. Even if there are no obvious indicators, keep your distance while you continue to talk, question and gather information. Some barotraumas can cause confusion and a feeling of exhaustion. Remain on alert for changes in the diver's manner and actions. The progression of some diving injuries rapidly accelerates and things may change from moment to moment.

If the diver requires your direct assistance, you'll need to be sure that both of you remain buoyant throughout the assist. Adjust both BCs so that you are both comfortable. The diver's state of mind and changes over the next couple of minutes will give you a good idea of the urgency of the situation. If you feel that his condition is deteriorating, then you could be justified in dropping his weight belt to reduce the drag. *Always* drop the victim's belt before you drop your own belt. Other clues may develop that indicate serious internal injuries such as excessive blood from the nose and mouth (though a small amount of blood from the nose may indicate a minor sinus squeeze), coughing, and the diver complaining of chest or abdominal pains.

This injured diver may become truly helpless in seconds. Protect his airway from spray and waves by cupping your hand over his nose and mouth. Don't pinch his nose and seal his mouth unless a wave is about to break over him. Always tell him what you're about to do this and advise him to hold his breath. You should start signaling for help as soon as you see signs that indicate more than just a tired or cold diver. You'll no doubt need help to remove the diver from the water, and could probably benefit from assistance during the tow. Look for help early on in the rescue which will not end until the diver is removed to safety and has been thoroughly evaluated.

Assess the circumstances as you approach the distressed diver.
• **Does he respond to your questions? Can he tell you what's wrong?**
• **Does his equipment appear to be intact? Is he floating high in the water because he dropped his weight belt? Is his BC over-inflated?**
• **Have the mask and regulator been discarded? Is he in danger of inhaling water?**
• **Is his breathing pattern abnormal? Coughing or choking? Bleeding from the nose or mouth?**

Unconscious Diver on the Surface

A diver on the surface who fails to respond is presumably in extreme danger. While your initial approach will be cautious, the victim's non-responsiveness even to touch, signals immediate assessment and life-saving action. Unconsciousness can be brought about by many means, drowning, barotraumas, hypothermia, and contaminated air supply. Breathing alterations may also lead to blackout. Whatever the cause, this is doubtless a life-threatening emergency, even if the victim is still breathing. Immediate action is required by the rescuer. Unconsciousness is always a medical emergency and will require attention from medical professionals.

A diver face down in the water and without a regulator or snorkel in his mouth is clearly not breathing. The first priority is to turn the diver face up. If you approach the diver from the side or legs, simply grab the BC and rotate him. His legs may be hanging below the surface if he's wearing a fabric or shell-type dry suit, making his body an "L" shape. You may need to push him for a stroke or two to get his legs to rise before he will roll. If you approach from the front, simply grasp his hand with your opposite hand (right to right or left to left) and pull him toward you. He'll rotate naturally into the face up position. Rescue breathing should be started immediately with two initiating breaths. Shout for assistance between breaths. Drop the victim's weight belt and add air as required to the BC. Fully inflating the BC will not be necessary without the weight belt and will just get in your way as you administer breaths. In an out-of-air situation, you may need to inflate the BC orally to a workable buoyancy level.

A diver face up in the water who remains unresponsive to direct contact may or may not be breathing when you arrive on scene. Determining breath signs may be very difficult in open water situations, even if the diver is not wearing a hood. Regardless, you should take a moment to look, listen and feel. The victim's skin color may be a good guide to respiration efficiency. A non-breathing or inadequately breathing person will be cyanotic (blue tinge to the skin), though this skin color will be evident in a hypothermic victim, even with (barely) adequate respirations. Whether the victim is not breathing at all or just barely, rescue breathing is called for. Persons with inadequate ventilations (that do not sufficiently oxygenate the brain and body tissues, thus the cyanosis), will benefit from rescue breathing. *You are unlikely to harm a breathing person by administering rescue breathing during an in-water rescue.*

Rescue breathing

A number of scuba diving accidents can lead to life-threatening emergencies. A non-breathing person in the water, whatever the cause, is an emergency where every second counts. Rapid and skillful rescue breathing may be the person's best chance for survival, and the most important talent a rescuer can bring to an in-water rescue. There's little doubt that the earlier that resuscitation efforts are begun, the more likely the victim will benefit. For this reason we will always try to commence rescue breathing as soon as we determine that the victim is not breathing. Except in circumstances where conditions are too rough or otherwise unsafe, or the transport to shore or the boat will take only a few seconds, waiting until we remove the victim from the water may be too long and the opportunity lost.

What we are attempting to do with in-water resuscitation is to ventilate the lungs of the non-breathing person by inflating their lungs with our exhaled breath. Despite the fact that we've already "used" this breath, there is still sufficient oxygen left in it to make this of value to a non-breathing person. Mouth-to-mouth resuscitation involves sealing the mouth of the victim with the rescuer's mouth, pinching the nose closed to prevent air escape, and exhaling a full breath into the (adult) victim. On the first exchange we deliv-

Look, listen, and feel to determine if a person is breathing. Skin color is a good clue to whether a person is breathing. A non-breathing victim will show cyanosis (blue tinge to the skin).

The earlier rescue breathing is started, the more likely the person will be resuscitated.

Find the rescue breathing technique that works best for you.

er two breaths, back to back, called initiating breaths. The victim's lungs will expel the air naturally after we deliver the breaths. On land we attempt to maintain a rhythm of one breath every 5 seconds (12 breaths/minute). In the water, this is much more difficult and, during a tow of the victim to safety, extremely demanding. A better rhythm for use in the water is two breaths every 10-12 seconds. This gives us more time to tow the victim, but still allows for adequate ventilations.

There are a couple of aspects of in-water resuscitation that the rescuer needs to keep in mind. First, to be effective the breaths must be clean and full exhalations. This means that we must make every effort to ensure that we do not blow any water into the victim's lungs and that they fully inflate. This can be difficult in poor surface water conditions, and will take considerable practice. Second, the breath exchanges early on in the resuscitation effort are probably the most important. It's worth the time to set up, relax and administer the breaths properly.

Improperly sealed mouth and nose, missed breaths, or blowing water into the lungs are an exercise in futility and waste valuable time. In some circumstances it may even make more sense to delay the tow until you have successfully completed several exchanges of breath. During a long tow you may become far too tired to breathe for anyone but yourself. The victim's ultimate survival in this case may well depend on how effectively you delivered those initial inflations. Third, delivering relatively fresh air to the victim's lungs does not automatically oxygenate the tissues.

In order to transport gases through the body, there must be a beating heart. Determining the presence or absence of a pulse in open water, not to mention the effect of the rescuer's own racing heart and mental state, is problematic at best. Therefore, we simply assume a beating heart until there is evidence to to demonstrate otherwise. While cardiac compressions can be performed in the water, these will most probably be ineffectual. In any case CPR is exceptionally difficult for one person to perform in the water

A final point for the rescuer to consider is the wisdom of performing actual mouth-to-mouth contact during rescue breathing. The recommendation of most professional life-saving agencies and emergency medical services is to employ a barrier or mask between the rescuer's mouth and the victim's mouth. This is a matter of prevention of disease transmission through orally-borne or blood-borne pathogens, as well as simple preference to avoid direct contact.

Pocket-type masks can be used in the water, though their application takes practice to use correctly. The principle problems are those of lack of obtaining a good seal around the mouth, and not enough hands to hold the victim, position his head, and hold the mask simultaneously. The best position for the rescuer is to stay at the head end and place the mask over the victim's face. Maintaining the mask in place throughout the rescue operation has the advantage of helping to keep water out of the victim's airway. Hold a finger over the air intake port to prevent the entry of water in rough or choppy sea conditions. Other barrier designs, particularly flat or strip types, are all useful, though not all are adaptable for in-water use.

Rescue breathing techniques

There is a large number of diver tow positions that a rescuer can use to bring a victim to safety. Only a couple, however, are really well suited to both towing and performing rescue breathing. Though the Do-Si-Do and "chin carry" are the most popular and, perhaps, the easiest to do, there are other techniques that may work equally well for you. Choose the one the gives you the best result in the greatest range of circumstances.

"Do-si-do" technique (pronounced Doe-see-Doe)

The Do-Si-Do technique (so-called because the divers link arms in a manner reminiscent of square dancing partners) can be performed from either the left or right side of the victim. Most right-handed people, however, find it easier to use the hand positions described below. Simply reverse the hands to use the Do-Si-Do from the other side.

1. Position the victim on his back in the water.
2. From the victim's left side, slide your left hand and arm between his left arm and his body.
3. Reach under the victim with your left hand to grasp the tank valve or collar of the exposure suit.
4. Rest your right hand on the victim's forehead to extend the neck

and keep the airway open.

5. Use your left hand and arm to roll the victim toward you sufficiently to begin mouth-to-mouth resuscitation. Use your right hand to pinch his nose closed as you exhale into the victim.

6. It is recommended that you stop swimming when delivering breaths to the victim. Position yourself to rise slightly in the water by bringing your fins back under you. This will give you better control.

7. If surface conditions are poor, use the right hand to cover the victim's nose and mouth to prevent aspiration of water.

Towing and manipulating the victim over anything but the shortest distance will always be much easier if the victim's scuba gear is first removed. Ensure that the unconscious, non-breathing victim is positively buoyant by dropping their weight belt. Use only enough air to maintain buoyancy and keep the victim's airway clear of water and spray. Note that putting too much

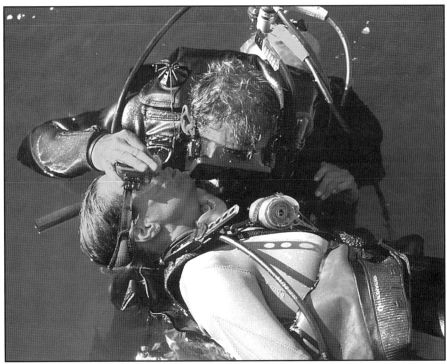

Rescue breathing is a valuable skill to have if the victim is non-breathing. Pinch the nose, seal the mouth, and start with two full initiating breaths, followed by 2 breaths every 10-12 seconds. Though the victim's mask might be removed in most cases, don't discard your own unless if interferes with your ability to deliver effective respiration.

air in the BC may make it difficult to get close enough to reach the victim to perform rescue breathing. This is true of your own BC as well. Once the victim's weight belt has been dropped, you may choose to release your own belt. As the tow progresses, you will probably want to ditch the victim's BC and tank, unless you cannot maintain sufficient buoyancy without them. Your own scuba unit will also impede your swim and should be ditched, especially on a long tow. An exception to this might be if surface conditions are so rough that you need to breathe regularly from your own scuba unit. In this case you wouldn't likely be performing rescue breathing anyway.

Note that many divers find the Do-Si-Do towing method quickly tiring and somewhat difficult to perform on a victim larger than themselves. The tow position is not very streamlined as the victim and rescuer are side by side. The Do-Si-Do does give the rescuer good control and allows for close monitoring of the victim. This is particularly important if the victim vomits during the tow or resuscitation effort. If this happens, roll the victim to keep his airway clear and be sure there is no residue left in the mouth.

Chin carry technique

The principle advantages of the "chin carry" method for towing and resuscitation is the increased speed with the rescuer can swim with the victim and the ease with which almost any rescuer can deliver effective rescue breathing. The rescuer and victim are in alignment and the rescuer is swimming on his back, allowing a very powerful fin stroke.

1. The rescuer makes the victim buoyant as described earlier.
2. The rescuer positions himself at the victim's head and uses the left hand, placed between the shoulder blades or center of the back, to provide enough lift to keep the victim clear of the water.
3. Grasping the victim's chin in his right hand, the rescuer cradles the victim's head on his right shoulder. Be careful with the hand placement so that it does not put pressure on the airway or carotid arteries.
4. To start rescue breathing, the rescue will slide the right hand up to the forehead to pinch the victim's nose closed during the breaths. The left hand must stay where it is to maintain sufficient lift.
5. When swimming, the rescuer slings his body under and in front of the victim. This permits rapid swimming and protects the helpless person from wave break. The right hand can easily be used to seal the nose and mouth to help keep water off the victim's face.

When in doubt, call for professional assistance.

Removing a diver from the water

Sometimes the most difficult part of a water rescue is removing a helpless person from the water. Even with a person's scuba equipment removed, the act of lifting and manipulating him can be an almost impossible task without adequate forethought and preparation. In some cases specialized equipment may be required to assist a diver with certain injuries. In all cases the rescuer will benefit from the ready hands of other qualified divers and support personnel. It's worth remembering, too, that the rescuer has possibly just performed a huge amount of work. Don't forget that the rescuer, maybe yourself, will need assistance to avoid becoming an exhausted/injured diver.

Backpack carry

When the rescuer reaches shore with the victim, he still faces the task of bringing him up onto the beach and away from the water. If all else fails, the rescuer could simply grasp the victim under the arms and walk backwards, dragging the victim behind him. In circumstances of a flat sloping beach and breaking surf, this may, in fact, be the only safe way to do this.

In almost all other situations, including rocky shores, it may be better to use the "backpack carry." Even a relatively small person can lift a large helpless person without much difficulty and perform a good "carry-out."

1. The rescuer stops the tow in water about mid-torso deep, takes off his fins and stands up.
2. Position the victim on his back with his head toward the shore or exit point.
3. For a right-handed rescuer it's best to stand on the victim's right side at about the victim's waist.
4. The rescuer reaches across to grasp the victim's his left wrist in his left hand, and holds the victim's right wrist in his right hand. If the

victim is so large that the rescuer's hands cannot hold
the wrists tightly enough, grab the thumbs or sleeves instead.

5. To be most effective, the rescuer will lift up on the victim's left arm while pushing down on the right. This will cause the victim to rotate around his own axis. Before the victim becomes face down in the water, however, the rescuer sinks his own body underwater and the victim will roll up on the rescuer's back.

6. The rescuer stays underwater while he adjusts the victim's position on his back. The key is to maneuver the victim to rest as high as possible with his arms over the rescuer's shoulders and crossed on the rescuer's chest. Done quickly and properly, the victim's face will not even get wet.

7. When the rescuer rises from the water, the victim will ride easily on his back and can be carried out of the water. In fact the rescuer will need only one hand to hold the victim and thus has a hand free to grab handholds there might be available.

8. The rescuer will gently lower the victim to the ground well above water level and remove the hood, if present, and check a carotid artery for the presence of a pulse.

A backpack carry is a surprisingly easy way to lift and remove a person from the water.

Turning the victim for the backpack carry.

Duck down into the water to position the victim.

The backpack carry may be the only way to move an unconscious or helpless person over a rocky shore.

Once on shore, look, listen, and feel for breath sounds.

Call for medical help anytime a diver becomes or has been unconscious.

If there are following seas or incoming waves during this lift, the rescuer should use the waves to help raise the victim onto his back. In circumstances where the waves are dangerously high, however, it would be wiser to wait for a lull between the breakers to do this, or any, lift. As always qualified assistants are a plus on any rescue scene.

Two-person carry

The presence of a second rescuer can greatly help in removing a person from the water. The two-person carry is an ideal way to use a second person to share the load and is quick to execute. The rescuers remove their fins and position themselves on either side of the victim. All three should be facing toward the shore. The rescuers will each drape one of the victim's arms over their own shoulders and wrap their victim-side arm around the victim's waist or back. The rescuers will then slide their free arms under the victim's legs and grasp each other's wrist. The victim will now be in a sitting position on the rescuers' arms with his back supported by their other arms. The rescuers will then simply walk out of the water to safety. When clear of the water, they will set the victim down gently and check for breathing and a pulse.

If you have assistance on shore, a two-person carry makes the load easier to carry and gives the rescuers more stability.

For a diver with a head, neck, or other serious injury, use a backboard or litter for transport to shore. Start by sinking the litter under the victim while a rescuer maintains control of the victim's airway and spine.

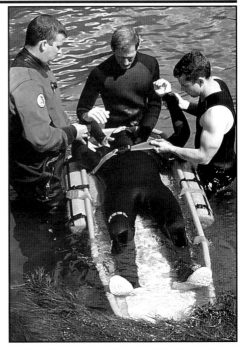

Always buckle the top strap first and ensure that it passes under the victim's arms. This helps prevent the victim from sliding down the board in case it has to be raised on an angle to get clear of the water.

In conditions of breaking waves and surf, it's entirely possible for a diver to be injured just getting in or out of the water. The same may also happen to rescuers attempting to remove a person from the water. Learn to use the waves as an aid to getting out of the water. Time your movements so that you're not constantly fighting the flow of water in and the backwash out. Plant your feet firmly as you feel the approach of the wave and brace yourself for the impact. Since both rescuers should move and stop together, it helps to have one of the rescuers call the stops and starts for both. If there is a third rescuer handy, it would be most advantageous for this person to keep the victim's head upright and to stabilize the neck. This gives more protection to a helpless person.

Recovering a person to a boat

Removing a helpless or unconscious person from the water and on to a boat can be a daunting task. Most dive boats are relatively high-sided, and you may not be able to reach the victim from the deck. Even inflatable boats can pose problems. Although they are low in the water, their "rail" is much wider than a standard boat, causing the rescuer to have to reach far out to pull the victim on board.

Unconscious person lift

To lift an unconscious person out of the water by hand calls more for good technique than strength. Position the victim as close as possible to the side of the inflatable to limit how far you have to reach. Most importantly, be sure to keep your center of gravity well within the boat to avoid falling overboard. Keep low and position the victim with his back to the boat. Reach under the victim's arms so the your arms are between the victim and the boat. This is important to limit the amount of friction generated between the two. Grasp the victim tightly and lift with your legs, not your back. It helps to wiggle the victim from side to side slightly, thereby lifting each side in increments. When you can brace your elbows on the top of the inflatable's side, use your legs to lift the victim until his waist is at the rail.

At this stage you can gently lower the victim to the deck, or even better, take a step back into the boat and the victim will trail along with you. As with all rescue techniques, this one will greatly improve with practice under experienced supervision. With a very heavy person two rescuers may be required. It will probably help to use a short length of rope to give the rescuers something easier to hold on to. Again start with the victim's back to the boat.

Even with an inflatable boat, removing an unconscious or helpless person from the water can be difficult. Keep your arms between the victim and the boat, and use your legs to lift the person clear of the rail of the boat.

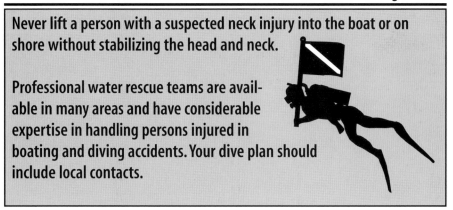

Never lift a person with a suspected neck injury into the boat or on shore without stabilizing the head and neck.

Professional water rescue teams are available in many areas and have considerable expertise in handling persons injured in boating and diving accidents. Your dive plan should include local contacts.

Pass the rope under one arm, around the chest and under the other arm. Cross the two ends of the rope behind the victim. Each rescuer will haul up on the end of rope nearest him until the victim is in the boat. The rescuers should pull away from each other during this lift to keep the rope tightly wrapped around the victim.

Roll-up net

Sometimes the victim is simply too heavy or the freeboard (height above waterline) is just too high to reach the victim. In these cases the rescuers might consider using some variation of a roll-up net. A tarp or blanket will also work well. Attach the inboard edge of the net to the rail or deck of the boat and drape the rest of the net in the water. Position the victim on his back in the water and pull him across the net. Reach to the outboard edge of the net and pull it back up to the boat. As the rescuers haul the net aboard, the victim will roll up in the net and up to the rail. At this stage remove the person from the net and gently lower him by hand to the deck.

If there is no net, tarp or suitable blanket on board, you might use a length of rope (about 20-25 ft. 6-8 m) in a pinch. Attach the two ends to the rail or deck, or stand on them, about 8 ft. (2.5 m) apart. Find the midpoint of the rope and attach it in a similar fashion. Now spread out the two "V"s on the water. Position the victim as described above across the Vs. Reach out to grab the points of the Vs and haul back as before. Be careful that the ropes do not cross the victim's neck during the lift. With a thick rope this technique is surprisingly comfortable for the victim.

The roll-up technique is generally fairly benign and will cause no further injury to an exhausted or near-drowning victim, though it should not be used if you suspect that the victim has a head or neck injury, or broken bones.

From a high-sided boat, or if the victim is particularly heavy, a roll-up net or some variation makes the lift a lot easier. In a pinch a tarp or a blanket can be used.

Boarding ladder

A high-sided dive boat will usually have a ladder to aid divers in the boarding after a dive. Obviously, an unconscious or seriously injured diver cannot climb the ladder unaided. Two well-known techniques for assisting an injured diver up a ladder are the "ladder carry," and the "BC carry." Just a quick word of caution, both of these techniques require considerable rescuer strength and practice.

The ladder carry starts with both rescuer and victim face to face at the foot of the ladder in the water, the rescuer stripped of all gear, the victim stripped of weight belt and scuba unit. The rescuer positions the victim's arms around his shoulders and wraps the victim's legs around his waist. The rescuer puts a foot on a rung of the ladder and uses that knee to support the victim. It helps if the victim can hold on. The rescuer climbs the ladder, one leg at a time, using arm strength.

The BC carry takes a minute to set up, but is a little more secure. The rescuer removes the tank and regulator attachments from the BC, but leaves the BC in place on the victim. Unbuckling any snaps or Velcro closures on the front of the BC, the rescuer essentially puts the BC on while the victim is still wearing it. If the BC can accommodate them both, the victim will be held snugly on the rescuer's back as he climbs the ladder. Again, arm and leg strength are important to accomplish this without injuring the rescuer or causing further harm to the victim.

Another method that may work if the rescuers cannot carry the victim up the ladder is to lower the ladder into the water and have the rescuer(s) tie the injured person the ladder. This is best done simply by positioning the injured person on his back on the ladder and running a single line from one side rail under the person's arms to the other side rail. Tie the line tightly to prevent the victim from sliding down during a vertical lift. Helpers on board the boat can then pull the ladder on board. This technique lends itself well where several people are available to assist, as ladders offer numerous hand-holds for multiple rescuers. It's also a good idea to test the flotation characteristics of the ladder as it's put in the water. A ladder that sinks quickly will need to be carefully tended while the victim is being secured to it.

Spine boards and flotation litters

Although we don't often think about head or neck injuries as being part of the water world that we inhabit as divers, there are plenty of opportunities for these kinds of accidents. From the strictly diving point of view, surfacing

A diver whom you suspect might have a head, neck, or other serious injury should always be stabilized on a backboard or litter, before lifting out of the water. If possible, you should get rescue professionals to assist with these operations.

divers have frequently been struck by the tending vessel or dive boat during pickups. Head, neck, collar bone and shoulder injuries are almost inevitable in these accidents. Head injuries also happen when boats bounce and roll in rough water, or when people on board lose their footing and fall to the deck. Any person falling off a large boat may also easily be seriously injured when striking the water. Whenever we suspect that there has been sufficient impact to cause a head, neck or "long bone" (e.g., thigh or upper arm) injury we should stabilize the patient within a litter or on a spineboard. Since this kind of equipment is not often carried on a dive boat, you will need to seek professional assistance from Coast Guard or local rescue teams. Remember that any time someone has had a period of unconsciousness for any reason you will need to summon medical assistance.

Useful rescue equipment

Throwable devices

Several items that can help to reach a diver some distance away from the boat, or to assist a rescuer towing a victim back to the boat are line-throwing devices. The most basic of these is the throw bag. This is a simple nylon bag containing from 50-75 ft (15-22 m) of floating polypropylene line. The rescuer opens the bag and holds the end of the line in the non-throwing hand. Using an underarm throw, the rescuer tosses the bag out to the person in the water. With surprisingly little practice, most people can send the bag out to the full extent of the line.

Any boat should have a life ring on board with from 75-125 ft. (22-38 m) of line attached. Though most people will have some difficulty tossing the ring more than 50 ft. (15 m), its greater flotation than a throw bag makes it strong contender for the most useful throwable device. Most life ring lines are hand-coiled or bound and will need to be "stacked or faked" before throwing the ring. Lay the ring on the ground or deck and unbind or uncoil the line. Starting at the free end, which is put to one side, feed the line into a small pile until you reach the ring. Before throwing the ring, hold or stand on the free end to prevent its loss. The ring itself is thrown with a side-arm motion with your throwing hand ending up pointing directly at the target.

A recent addition to the throwing-aid arsenal is the Rescue Disc®. Built along the lines of a double-thickness Frisbee®, the disc has 75 ft. (22 m) of polypropylene line wrapped around it. The device is thrown exactly like a Frisbee and can easily reach a considerable distance. The Rescue Disc® is affected by wind direction and strength, so practice is recommended.

For greater distances, some rescue teams use line-throwing guns of one kind or another. Increasingly popular because it does not use rifle shells or explosive devices is the Rescue Rocket®. This device is charged with compressed air from, for example, a scuba cylinder and can carry a line out to several hundred feet. A special attachment allows the rocket on the end to be replaced by a self-inflating life ring.

Swimmer devices

Seeing a diver in distress on the surface, a swimmer could deploy from shore or boat to assist. There would be great advantage in carrying a small flotation device in these cases to give to a panicky diver for additional buoyancy or a device for towing. A common example of a portable flotation device is a rescue can, sometimes called a "torpedo." Shaped like a flattened cone with handles, these devices are easily towed by a swimmer who wears a tether line connected to the device. The rescue can is designed to be grasped by a struggling victim, but in skilled hands can also be used as a flotation device. Positioning the can under the victim's upper back will give considerable buoyancy to a helpless person and make them much easier to tow.

A "rescue tube" is also a valuable aid in water rescue. Made of soft foam under a tough vinyl skin, the tube is looped around the victim to provide immediate flotation assistance. Also connected by a tether to the swimmer, it greatly reduces anxiety on the part of a conscious person and can fully float an unconscious person. It has the added advantage of being a useful in-water tool for immobilizing a cervical spine (neck) injury.

Consider taking a personal flotation device (PFD) with you if you swim out to a diver in distress. Handing the PFD to the victim will allow you to keep clear of flailing arms and legs, and give the victim enough additional flotation that the panic may quickly pass on its own. You can then hold the far side of the PFD and use it to tow the diver back to safety.

Personal considerations

The ability to perform these rescue techniques is not something that is easily accomplished the first time out. Though not complicated in themselves, all techniques for handling another person in situations that are both physically challenging and stressful require practice and refinement. The basic requirement for the rescuer is to be fully comfortable himself in the water. The physical fitness component necessary to perform a rescue should be obvious. Even in a pool it is tiring to tow another person 100 yd. (90 m). Once these techniques have been mastered, improvement will come from practicing them in increasingly difficult conditions, the very conditions most likely to produce a diving accident. With increased skill comes greater confidence, a combination that makes the dive rescue specialist an invaluable asset in any dive party.

Scuba I.Q. Review

1. What signs might signal to an observer that a diver on the surface may be in distress?

2. Why is a reaching or throwing response the preferred way of assisting a diver to shore or to the boat?

3. Why is it prudent to stop at least 15 ft. (5 m) away from a diver whom you think might be having problems?

4. Why is panic the leading cause of diver accidents?

5. What are the best steps to follow in assisting a panic or struggling diver?

6. The most likely rescue scenario in aiding a fellow diver is...?

7. An unconscious, breathing diver on the surface is in extreme danger of...?

8. How do we determine if a person is breathing?

Notes

Chapter 5
Responding to Emergencies Underwater

Responding to Emergencies Underwater

By its very nature scuba diving exposes us to risks associated with being underwater. The hyperbaric (high pressure) environment in which we function has hazards of its own and, combined with temperature considerations, physical hazards such as currents, entangling dangers, and even hostile marine life, we understand that there is always the possibility of an underwater accident. Despite all this, the most common factor in an accident remains poor judgment on the part of the diver(s). Learning to recognize and respond to these diving incidents is the objective of this chapter.

Recognizing underwater hazards
Accident prevention

We already know that pre-dive preparation is our best hedge against being overtaken by the unexpected while underwater. We plan the dive according to what we expect the underwater environment to be and what we intend to accomplish on the dive. We figure the route, air consumption factors, maximum depth and time and so on. On the dive itself we superimpose the image of the route over our actual course, so we have a good idea of exactly where we are at any given time. Still, the dive doesn't often keep strictly to plan.

We constantly fine-tune the plan as we go along because of the realities of the dive. Such things as changing currents, thermoclines, surge, and encountering areas of particular interest that require more than a cursory glance, all may conspire to make a shambles of the original plan. This is not a problem in itself. After all, spontaneity is a virtue, not a vice. Awareness of the effect that such alterations may produce on important dive parameters such as depth limitations, air rationing and bottom times, however, is critical to good diving. Awareness is, in fact, the key ingredient to accident avoidance, which is why the self-reliant diver is usually a better diver.

Having adequately prepared for the dive, accident prevention underwater will ultimately depend on our ability to pay attention to ourselves, our buddies and our environment. Rare is the accident report that states that the diver was struck by a falling anchor or buried in an underwater earthquake or electrocuted by an trans-oceanic power cable. In the end, mishaps will almost always come from our actions, inactions or reactions.

Signs of trouble underwater

A good diver learns to recognize those things that indicate a diver at ease in the environment and in their personal comfort zone. A diver may unintentionally signal a growing sense of unease to the alert buddy. Common indicators of stress are erratic movement and breathing patterns.

A diver who experiences apparent difficulty with buoyancy control, orientation or maintaining buddy contact may not be concentrating on the dive. This could be caused by several factors such as cold, fear, weighting problems or confusion. At depth we might add nitrogen narcosis and poor equipment performance to this list. Breathing pattern alterations produce or indicate problems, too. Exceptionally slow breathing or rapid breathing may be the result of other problems or, conversely, can cause physiological changes in the diver that may lead to panic or unconsciousness.

Buoyancy control is of particular importance in "blue water" diving, that is, when diving over deep, open water. Boat diving near a reef or wall with a deep drop-off is such an example. Poor buoyancy control may result in rapid changes in depth which in turn can cause ear and mask squeezes, too rapid descents resulting in excessive depths and too rapid ascents resulting in over-

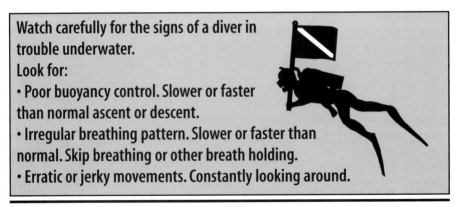

Watch carefully for the signs of a diver in trouble underwater.
Look for:
• Poor buoyancy control. Slower or faster than normal ascent or descent.
• Irregular breathing pattern. Slower or faster than normal. Skip breathing or other breath holding.
• Erratic or jerky movements. Constantly looking around.

exertion to stay down and in dangers to the lungs due to expanding air. A diver "bouncing" up and down should be watched carefully and assisted to achieve neutral buoyancy. More serious problems may be imminent unless the diver regains control, or his buddy intervenes.

Underwater emergencies

Diver emergencies can happen at any depth and at any stage of the dive. They can happen to novices and to experienced divers, in calm conditions or in turbulent waters. A timely response will depend on our recognition that something is wrong and a working knowledge of the signs these emergencies present.

Entangled diver

Diver-entanglement incidents are neither that unusual nor as life-threatening as the novice diver might believe. It takes only a moment's inattention for a diver to swim into an anchor line, buoy line or long, thick strands of kelp. Any of these and more may cause a diver to become hung up. The chief culprits here are the tank valve and dangling gauges and hoses. Interestingly, most divers get snagged and spend several seconds or more finning, never suspecting that they're making little or no progress, since lines and kelp have enough "give" in them to create the illusion of forward movement. Divers who belatedly realize that they're caught often react with impatience, rolling from side to side or else swimming up. Both of these reactions typically result in further entangling the victim.

The watchwords in this and any other underwater predicament are always *Stop* your activity, keep your *Self-Control* and consider your *Options*. Kelp strands, for example, seems to have the remarkable and irritating ability to wrap more tightly as the diver struggles against them. Instead of thrashing at inanimate objects, the diver would do much better to stop and back out or relax completely and float out of the kelp bed. This lesson in self-rescue holds true for almost any other circumstance a diver might encounter. The only real exception might be a monofilament fishing net (gill net). Though these are not very common anymore, they are still used in some areas. Constructed to be invisible underwater, an unwary diver could blunder into one and not realize it until well tangled. Absolute buoyancy control is required to prevent further tangling while you retrieve and use the dive knife to free yourself. You may even have to remove the scuba unit as you do this as the tank valve and first stage of the regulator are the most likely objects to snag.

Prevention is always preferable to rescue. Seeing your buddy about to swim unawares into a line or other snag, you would save him frustration and anxiety by warning him. If your buddy does get caught, your first task is to keep him calm. With the advantage of being able to see what exactly is holding the diver in place, it will probably only take you a moment to disentangle him. Rarely will it be necessary to cut anything, if you can get the diver simply to back up and out of the kelp or line. In lakes and large ponds, however, it's not at all unusual to accidentally drag along nylon fishing lines which have the peculiar habit of snagging on fin straps and wrapping around your feet. A good, line-cutting knife is usually the quickest solution and, leaving the line in small pieces, prevents another diver from making the same mistake.

Lack of adequate hydration is a contributing factor to hypothermia, hyperthermia, and decompression sickness.

Carotid sinus reflex

Humans are terrestrial, rather than naturally aquatic animals. One of the consequences of this has been that our bodies have adapted to changes in the way gravity affects our circulation depending on whether we're standing upright or lying down. To function properly we need to have nearly constant blood pressure to all parts of our body.

The brain, in particular, is very sensitive to changes in blood flow as this determines the amount of oxygen the brain receives. The "measuring gauges" for blood flow to the brain are in the carotid arteries. These large arteries are found on either side of the windpipe and are the source of the pulse we feel in the front of the neck. Specifically, the pulse is the carotid artery sinus, an enlarged space in the arteries themselves. This measuring device determines the correct pressure of blood to deliver to the brain, depending on the body's position.

These sinuses can be tricked, however, if external pressure is applied to the carotid arteries or to the sinuses themselves. If this happens, then the sinuses will react by signaling for a reduction in the blood pressure and, thus, the oxygen to the brain. In the diving environment this can come about if the wet suit hood or jacket collar is too tight, or if the neck seal of a dry suit is constrictive. Even if normal wear of these items is not all that uncomfortable, we can sometimes bring the condition on by craning our head back to look straight up in the water. This may cause increased pressure in the carotid arteries which in turn will lead to a drop in blood pressure.

The diminished flow of oxygen to the brain has an immediate effect. The diver will feel sudden bouts of dizziness and vertigo. Since this seems to come out of nowhere, completely without warning and evident cause, it can be a frightening experience. The sensation will pass quickly, however, when the diver looks down, restoring normal blood flow to the brain. *Sudden blackout can occur in extreme cases*, one of the very few ways this may happen to a scuba diver on the bottom.

Carbon monoxide (CO) gas poisoning

As scuba divers we're completely dependent on our breathing mixture while underwater. We depend on the fact that the air meets the stringent standards necessary for us to stay healthy and functional under pressure. One of the most critical measures of impurities in breathing air is the amount of CO, carbon monoxide, present in the air we breathe. Because we will always have more air in our lungs while underwater than we'd have if we were on the surface, trace gases that would be acceptable in normal breathing air will be unacceptable on scuba. For scuba air a level of only 0.001% CO is permitted.

CO is odorless, colorless and tasteless, thus impossible to detect in the air. Since it is produced by incomplete combustion, however, the air may have an associated taste that could alert the diver. Typically, CO gets into the scuba cylinder when the intake to the compressor used to fill the tank is too close to exhaust from vehicles or smoke sources. In some cases it may be produced in the compressor itself if the high pressure stage of the compressor is "burning" oil. In all these cases there is the possibility that the diver may detect an oily or smoky taste, but there is no guarantee of this.

CO is dangerous because it binds so readily to the hemoglobin molecule in red blood cells. In fact it has a much greater affinity for hemoglobin than oxygen has. This means that CO will attach to hemoglobin more quickly than O_2 will. To make matters worse, CO stays attached to the red blood cells far longer than oxygen does. Oxygen exchanges readily throughout the body in those tissues that require it. CO stays attached for up 5-6 hours before

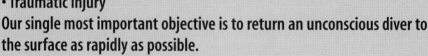

Unconsciousness underwater may be due to several factors:
- Carbon monoxide poisoning
- Hypothermia
- Drowning
- Lung over-expansion injuries
- Nitrogen narcosis
- Carotid sinus reflex
- Out-of-air emergency
- Marine life injury
- Traumatic injury

Our single most important objective is to return an unconscious diver to the surface as rapidly as possible.

releasing itself from hemoglobin. For this period of time, the hemoglobin of the affected red blood cells is effectively out of action.

For the diver the effects of CO poisoning underwater are insidious. The gradual accumulation of CO-bound red blood cells causes a gradual diminishing of O_2 transport throughout the body. Still this drop in O_2 level in the red blood cells is compensated for to some extent by the increased partial pressure of O_2 the diver receives in the air he breathes. Even though the hemoglobin is increasingly bound by CO the elevated PO_2 in the lungs allows the plasma and other fluids to absorb more O_2 than usual. This O_2 is transported throughout the body as easily as if were attached in the red blood cells and mitigates the effects of CO poisoning to some extent, as long as the diver stays on the bottom. As the diver ascends, probably assailed by headache, tightness across the forehead, and feeling a little "dopey", the PO_2 drops to more normal levels. Suddenly the diver is starved of oxygen on the way up. At the surface or shortly afterward, the diver may face a real crisis as the red blood cells cannot provide sufficient oxygen to keep the brain and vital organs supplied. Collapse may be sudden and catastrophic. Recall that CO may stay attached to hemoglobin for 5-6 hours, and the peril to the victim is clear.

The on-scene treatment of choice is pure oxygen, delivered through a non-rebreather mask at the highest possible flow rates. There are two benefits to this treatment. First, breathing pure oxygen raises the PO_2 of the circulating blood by the same process as took place while the diver was underwater. This allows oxygenation of tissues that the red blood cells are no longer able to supply in the normal way. We can literally keep the brain and body alive in this way, even without a large number of CO-bound red blood cells participating. A second important benefit is that a high level of O_2 helps to flush CO from the body much more quickly than would normally occur. Instead of a 5-6 hour turn-over time for CO, this can be reduced to as little as 1-11/2 hours. The definitive treatment is hyperbaric oxygen as can be administered in a recompression chamber. In this case the CO binding time can be cut back to 30 minutes.

On scene we must be prepared to support both ventilations and circulation by CPR, if necessary. Rapid transport to medical facilities is essential, even if the patient seems to have recovered. There may be serious long-term consequences of CO poisoning that must be treated by medical professionals. Also, be sure to secure the diver's equipment for later examination. The air must be tested for purity. Note that it's certainly possible for several divers on scene to have had air fills from the same suspect compressor. *No one who had a fill from the same station as the victim can be permitted to use those tanks until the air has been tested.*

Unconsciousness underwater may be caused by several problems. Approach a non-moving diver carefully and attempt to rouse them by gently shaking them.

Chapter 5
Nitrogen narcosis

One of the most fascinating, and fabled, aspects of scuba diving is the phenomenon known as nitrogen narcosis. Layered with doubtful stories of buddy-breathing with fish and accounts of mermaid sightings, and of its incompletely understood cause, the truth behind narcosis is considerably less dramatic.

Narcosis is certainly related to the depth of the dive and to the gases we breathe. Dives deeper than 100 ft. (30 m) will induce many recreational divers not accustomed to this depth to begin to demonstrate the effects of narcosis. At this depth, the effects are subtle and may not even be evident to the diver or buddy. Tests of fine motor skills or problem solving may show some deficits, but on a normal dive with normal activities, these deficits will likely be missed.

At depths greater than 150 ft. (45 m) the effects become more pronounced and many divers will feel and demonstrate more overt reactions. Narcosis passes quickly, however, as the diver rises to shallower depths, and disappears completely on ascent. That narcosis is caused by the nitrogen in the breathing air is also beyond dispute. This is surprising since we understand nitrogen to be an inert gas, that is, it doesn't combine or react with other compounds easily. The most widely accepted theory for nitrogen's effect is that it is readily soluble in fat tissue at high pressures. Some of the tissue absorbing nitrogen, then, would be parts of nerve cells' natural wiring that connects nerve cells together. It is theorized that this absorption interferes with nerve signal transmission, resulting in delays and misfiring between cells in the nervous system.

Interestingly, nitrogen is not the only gas that causes narcosis, and not even the worst. Argon and other inert gases have more severe effects than nitrogen, while others such as helium have far less effect. It's for this reason that divers who use mixed gases for the more extreme dives will substitute much of the nitrogen with helium. Even though any inert gas can cause decompression sickness (including helium), narcosis poses a greater risk to the prepared deep diver than does decompression sickness. It's worth noting that experienced deep water divers concur that a certain amount of adaptation to narcosis occurs with frequent deep dives. This is another strong argument for advanced training and greater than normal experience before undertaking the more extreme dives.

The effects of narcosis are proportional to depth, but, generally within sport diving ranges, the most commonly reported are:
- Euphoria
- Decreased manual dexterity

- Light headedness
- Diminished problem solving ability
- Fixation
- Hallucinations

To make this list even more interesting, many divers experience a certain amount of amnesia after the dive, thus do not remember or else deny their odd behavior. Factors that seem to predispose divers to narcosis include:

- Rapid descent
- Heavy exertion at depth (resulting in CO_2 retention)
- Cold water
- Alcohol or other drugs
- Apprehension (may be brought on by low visibility or other circumstances)
- Pre-existing fatigue (late nights, hard work)

Our role as a rescuer in these situations has to be, first and foremost, one of remaining vigilant to the signs of narcosis in ourselves or our buddy. We must recognize that this is not an amusing situation. A diver suffering the effects of narcosis is a danger to himself and any others on the dive. Bear in mind that divers may find themselves at depth unintentionally. Diving along steep walls that fall off to great depth, cruising with whales or dolphins in blue water or being moved off reefs by currents may all result in much deeper than intended dive profiles. The utter tranquillity and beauty of many dive sites may capture the diver's attention when in fact he should be looking at his depth gauge. It can and does happen to the best of divers.

Ascent is the only real solution to narcosis. Signal your buddy to go up until you see that the effects of narcosis have passed. Be insistent, if necessary, but attempting to take control of your buddy's equipment by inflating his BC or dropping his weight belt are *not* good responses. Your buddy might resist your interference with dire consequences for you both, or if successful, you may send your buddy uncontrolled to the surface from great depth.

Nitrogen narcosis can be an incapacitating event for a diver at depths greater than 100 feet (30m). Develop your deep diving skills slowly to help get adapted to the demands of depth.

Squeezes

The most common direct effects of pressure for scuba divers are squeezes, or the compression of discrete air spaces in the body. This is a consequence of the simple pressure/volume relationships that acts upon almost all aspects of diving. Numerous such air spaces exist in the body, the middle and outer ears, the sinuses, and the lungs. External to the body, but in contact with the skin, are other air spaces. Examples of these are between the mask and face, under the diver's hood, and within a dry suit.

If you fail to equalize the pressure inside your mask you can suffer a "squeeze."

Ear squeeze

By far the most likely injury a diver will ever experience is a middle ear squeeze. The middle ear is an air space between the ear drum on the outside and the eustachian tube on the inside. The eustachian tube leads directly to the back of the throat, another air space. At normal atmospheric pressure on the surface, the air pressure in the middle ear is the same as the ambient or surrounding pressure.

As we descend underwater, the pressure builds up around us faster than it can be equalized in the middle ear. This results in an imbalance of pressure outside pressing on the ear drum and causing it to flex inward. The diver experiences this first as discomfort and then as outright pain. Unless the diver undertakes corrective action to equalize these pressures as the descent continues, the external pressure may bring about a rupture or perforation of the drum. Water will then flood into the middle ear, drawn by the relative vacuum inside.

The pain of this squeeze cannot be ignored by the diver, who will always react to restore the equilibrium. In most cases it becomes increasingly difficult to correct the problem the longer the diver waits to take action. For this reason we should always suggest to the diver having apparent difficulties with equalizing pressures to ascend a few feet. The drop in external pressure as the

Early and often are the key words for clearing your ears on descent. Learn several methods of equalizing pressures to ensure complete clearing, while sparing excess work on your ear drums.

diver rises will make it easier to clear his ears by reducing the pressure differential. Relaxation also helps. A diver who is tense and in a hurry will have a harder time equalizing than one who is deliberate and calm. In any case slower descents are always better than rapid ones.

Early, frequent and continuous efforts to minimize the imbalance will prevent most incidents of middle ear squeeze, but a diver who is over-weighted or who has poor buoyancy control may descend too quickly to equalize properly. If a perforation or rupture takes place and water enters the middle ear, it will come into contact with the inner ear "windows." These membranes cover openings to the hearing and balance mechanisms of the inner ear. This may have a drastic effect on the diver's ability to orientate himself underwater. The colder the water, the greater the effect. The diver may, in fact, be trying to swim to the surface, but because of his lack of balance and orientation, he may not be able to swim in the correct direction, even if he can see his destination.

Clearly our role as a rescuer is to prevent the diver from panicking and swimming off in the wrong direction. The best course of action is to calm the victim and assist him to get back to the surface at the recommended ascent rate. On the surface he may still require help to swim back to shore or the dive boat. Much of the effect will wear off over the next few minutes, however, as the water warms to body temperature; it's the temperature shock that disorients the diver.

On the surface there may be some blood evident in the diver's outer ear from the ear drum. Cover the ear canal with a clean dressing to help limit the chances of infection. The diver will need to seek medical attention for definitive care which will probably include staying out of the water for at least a month or two. Beyond this, there is rarely a more serious outcome to this accident. The drum normally heals well and will not often result in any compromise to hearing in the long run.

Chapter 5
Reverse squeeze

Once at depth and fully equalized, a diver's ears will have air in the middle ear at the same pressure as the water around him. On ascent the water pressure surrounding the diver begins to drop, making the air in the middle ear at a higher pressure than the surroundings. Fortunately, the diver rarely has to pay much attention to this imbalance as the excess pressure in the middle ear seeps naturally down the eustachian tube and into the back of the throat. In fact many divers often wonder why the air exhausts so easily from the middle ear, but requires direct intervention on the part of the diver to get into the middle ear. The reason is that the end of the eustachian tube at the back of the throat is covered by a one-way valve which naturally opens outward. Air easily pushes out of the eustachian tuba and middle ear, but must work past the one-way valve to get in.

Most experienced divers know that using the Valsalva method of equalizing pressures during multiple ascents and descents on a dive will eventually cause pain in the ears. This is because artificially increasing the internal air pressure in the throat forces the valve inwards, not its natural direction. While this *does* push the high pressure into the middle ear, it comes at a price. Over frequent episodes of ear clearing by this method, the valve and surrounding tissues become irritated and swollen. This in turn may precipitate problems later in the dive. There are much better and gentler ways of ear clearing with which divers should be accustomed.

On ascent anything that prevents or slows the escape of the relatively high pressure air from the middle ear will cause discomfort and pain. The culprit here is the high pressure air pushing *outward* on the ear drum in an effort to escape. Failure to drain this air back through the eustachian tube may well result in a perforated or torn ear drum on ascent. This failure of air to escape in the normal fashion results from several possibilities. The most common circumstance is when a diver is diving with a head cold. Mucous, blown into the eustachian tube, may plug the outlet and trap the air inside the middle ear. Also, too forceful and frequent Valsalvas may produce so much irritation and inflammation that the end of the eustachian tube swells shut.

Typically, the reverse block or squeeze comes at an unfortunate time for the diver. He's probably at the end of the dive and low on air, a bit chilly and ready to get out of the water. Ascending higher only exacerbates the problem since it results in a greater differential between the ambient and internal pressures. In fact there is no simple, foolproof way of dealing with this problem. The best advice to give the diver is to descend again until the pain disappears or at least lessens. From this depth the diver should ascend slowly, allowing sufficient time for the growing pressure in the middle ear to force the blockage out. This may have to be repeated several times. Swallowing may be helpful, too, as the pressure fluctuations this produces in the throat can aid the plug in moving. Even if the diver is successful in surfacing without causing an ear drum injury, he may complain of muffled hearing or "water in the ear" or stuffiness in the ear after the dive. This is the residue of high pressure air that did not escape and remains trapped in the middle ear. While this will pass over time, anywhere from a few minutes to days after the dive, it does likely indicate that the diver should not undertake any further diving until the underlying issue, that head cold and runny nose, has been completely eradicated. Decongestants and antihistamines will help clear away these effects sooner. Never take these drugs *prior* to a dive.

Sinus squeezes

The sinuses are four sets of hollow areas in the skull bones. As they are all air-containing spaces, they are subject to the same changes in pressure as the ear passages. The sinuses themselves are lined with mucous membranes which are themselves well supplied with blood vessels. Each sinus is connected to the nasal passages or throat by its own air passage through the bone. Normally these air spaces are equalized at the same time the diver equalizes his ears, and rarely present themselves as a problem. Diving with a cold or when suffering from an allergy or other infection, however, may block these passages and not permit one or more sinus to equalize properly. If this happens on descent, the relative vacuum in the sinus may rupture small blood vessels and fill the sinus with fluid. Depending on which sinus is affected, the diver will feel discomfort and pain in different places in the skull.

Most commonly, the maxillary sinuses are blocked. These are located just above the teeth and on either side of the nose. Divers sometimes confuse this pain with a 'tooth' squeeze which is a rare and a different condition altogether. A tooth squeeze results from the effects of pressure on a pocket of air under a filling in a tooth. The filling should have been packed tightly so that no air was left, but air will sometimes seep between it and the tooth. Pressurized air left remaining in this tiny space on ascent has been known to actually crack the tooth or even cause it to explode.

Often a sinus squeeze occurs and the diver felt no significant sensation at all. The only evidence that it occurred is the presence of blood in the mask after the dive. In some cases the diver may complain of a headache, depending on which sinus or sinuses were affected and whether any high pressure remains trapped after the dive. A common dive site remedy for this condition and for reverse ear squeezes is to take antihistamines or decongestants before the dive to clear, dry and open the air passages. *This is not a safe practice.* These drugs have side effects that can effect the diver's performance underwater and increase the risk of other injuries. In addition these drugs may wear off while the diver is still underwater, putting him in a very difficult position for the ascent. *TDI/SDI policy does not recommend taking these or any other drugs prior to diving.*

Equipment squeezes

Our diving equipment encloses air spaces against our body from the outside. These air spaces are subject to compression, or squeezes, as the diver descends in the water column, just as the internal air spaces are. The resulting partial vacuum effects the body part directly underneath the piece of equipment and may result in injury.

Mask squeeze

The increase in ambient pressure on descent may cause a diving mask to squeeze ever more tightly to the diver's face. The effect of this suction on the diver's face is clear to see after the dive. Often the diver has blood-shot eyes from burst blood vessels, perhaps a nosebleed and in extreme cases the diver's face may look bruised. There may not be any pain associated with this, but the results are often unsightly.

This whole syndrome is an unexpected offshoot of a mask that fits *too* well. Most of us have to clear some water out of our masks from time to time and thus introduce ambient pressure into the mask. Divers who feel the pressure building on the mask will thus deliberately exhale air into the mask to prevent the squeeze. This is of particular importance to breath-hold divers who have limited time to descend and may pay less attention to mask equalizing. Any diver, however, is subject to mask squeezes.

Dry suit squeeze

Dry suits trap an insulating layer of air within the special dry suit undergarments worn by the diver, creating a warmer environment for its wearer. This also allows the diver to vary his insulation in colder or warmer water. This in turn traps more air and increases the insulating quality of the suit. This air space is also subject to compression as the diver descends in the water. Unless the diver acts to add air to the suit, the fabric of the suit and even the clothing may be pressed tightly to the diver's skin, much like a vacuum-packed food item. Divers who use their BC to control their buoyancy, rather than add air to the suit for buoyancy, may suffer a suit squeeze that

If you are not properly trained, you can experience a "squeeze" when using a dry suit.

Photo courtesy of Scubapro

leaves bruises on the skin. The bruising is the result of blood vessels under the skin that burst due to suction directly on the skin.

Most authorities recommend using the dry suit for buoyancy control underwater, and the BC for surface flotation and back-up for beginning divers. Adding air to the suit for buoyancy purposes has the advantage of also maintaining the insulating layer at the original thickness, keeping the diver warmer. In addition, on ascent the diver need vent only suit air to control the ascent rate.

Experienced dry suit divers who choose to add air to the BC underwater must also remember to add some air to the suit to prevent a squeeze and to retain at least some of the insulating properties of the undergarments. They must also remember to vent both the BC *and* the excess air in the suit on ascent. Managing two buoyancy compartments underwater is considered an advanced skill.

Adding air to both the dry suit and BC underwater has lead to numerous rapid ascent situations among already task-loaded divers. A growing number of professional divers have concluded, therefore, that the BC should be used for additional surface flotation only, except in those cases where additional buoyancy may be required in an underwater situation.

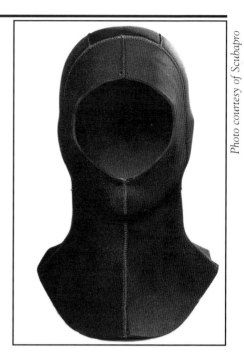

Photo courtesy of Scubapro

A snug fitting hood can cause a squeeze, too.

Hood squeeze

In order for the diver to equalize external ear pressures correctly, water must enter the diver's hood. If this does not happen, the hood will be forced into the outer ear by external pressure, but will never be able to effectively transfer the exact or full ambient pressure since there is still air trapped in the outer ear. This is typically a greater problem with dry suit divers who tend to use hoods which have tight-fitting "skin-seals" around the face and similar seals to mate more intimately with the dry suit neck seal. Divers who wear latex hoods and employ full-face masks run the same risk. To be able to effectively equalize external ear pressure, the diver must force air past the face seal into the hood.

Major barotraumas- Decompression illness

Technically, the term "barotrauma" refers to any pressure related injury. Thus, though the squeezes just discussed are really barotraumas, the term is equally used for those most serious and potentially life-threatening diving injuries; i.e., lung over-expansion injuries, and decompression sickness. Prevention, early recognition and appropriate on-scene treatment will greatly aid in averting long-term consequences.

The term "DCS" - decompression sickness - is more properly used to describe the "bends." The term "DCI"- decompression illness - is used to describe cases that have features of both DCS and "AGE" - arterial gas embolism - caused by a lung over-expansion injury.

Decompression sickness

Popularly known as the "bends," decompression sickness or DCS is caused by the rapid release of nitrogen held in solution by higher than normal ambient pressure. This nitrogen is that portion of the air that the diver breathed at depth and which dissolved in the tissues and blood. Basic gas laws tell us that the greater the ambient pressure, the greater the amount of gas will dissolve in liquid. As long as the diver remains under pressure, the absorbed gas will stay in solution, even as more is absorbed. This applies to all divers regardless of their depth and how long they stay. On ascent the nitrogen will leave its dissolved state and be exhaled. It's literally true that a diver exhales less air than he breathes in while at depth, and breathes out more than he inhales on ascent.

The problem arises when the diver ascends faster than his body can recover and exhale nitrogen from his system. In this case, the nitrogen will form bubbles in the tissues and blood. Since these bubbles are collected on the return portion of the circulation, DCS is a condition of venous gas embolism. Where the bubbles travel and how many of them form will determine the severity of the decompression sickness "hit." It should be emphasized that rate of ascent is one of the most important factors in precipitating DCS. Most dive computers currently recommend an ascent rate of approximately 30 ft./minute, although some may be faster or slower. A slow ascent rate really just gives the diver's physiology time to catch up with the physics.

All divers understand that we operate under no-decompression rules which limit the time we may spend at any particular depth and still allow us to ascend at a normal ascent rate. Exceeding those limits, as may happen on repetitive dives or especially deep dives, requires a stop for decompression at pre-set depths and duration. What these stops actually do is slow our ascent rate so that in fact our physiology *can* catch up with the physics. *Always ascend at a slow, controlled rate and make a safety stop at 15ft. (5 m) for three minutes.*

On-going research into the exact mechanisms of bubble formation and transport in the body have revealed decompression sickness to be a highly complex condition. What has become clear, however, is that there are several positively pre-disposing factors to its incidence, and that this susceptibility is variable between individuals. In general it's agreed that dehydration makes a diver more susceptible to DCS, as it does to hypothermia and heat-related injuries. Breathing very dry scuba air, especially if working hard underwater, will dehydrate a diver quickly.

Working hard will itself increase the chances of DCS by maintaining high concentrations of nitrogen-rich air in the lungs and increasing the circulation rate. In fact, anything that affects the physical health of the diver underwater, such as poor physical condition, habitual heavy smoker, abuse of alcohol or other drugs, and tiredness before the dive can increase the risk of decompression sickness, as well as other risks. Generally, older divers are more at risk due to the gradual deterioration of respiratory and circulatory systems. Since adipose (fat) tissue has a special affinity for dissolved nitrogen, obese individuals are also at increased risk of DCS.

Conditions of the dive will bear on the likelihood of DCS, as well. In particular cold-water diving results in the absorption and retention of more nitrogen. Again, the gas laws tell us that cold liquids will hold more dissolved gas than will warm liquids. As the diver chills, and this is especially true of the blood circulating just under the skin, more N_2 can be held in solution, thus increasing the body's total nitrogen load.

Divers operating in cold water are advised to decrease their projected no-decompression limits accordingly. This applies, too, to those divers exerting themselves during the dive. The presence of currents, extra distances to swim and carrying loaded game bags or photo equipment will cause divers to fall into this category and call for more conservative bottom times. *If facing both cold water and heavy work load, divers need to compensate for both.*

Most divers are careful enough to plan their dives taking into account the effect of bottom time and decompression sickness. Though many divers use dive tables which give guidelines for maximum bottom times at any given depth, increasingly divers are trained in the use of dive computers, and a majority of divers own one. Whether using dive tables or computers, divers are cautioned not to extend their dive times to the limit displayed. Individual variability, which may change even from one day to the next, means that no dive is ever completely without some risk.

DCS recognition

Aside from preventing DCS through cautious and considered diving practice, our principle concern as rescue-trained divers is the recognition and on-scene treatment of decompression sickness. In part, knowing the history or witnessing the event will give us much important information to help us determine the likelihood that any set of signs and symptoms indicates DCS. For example, knowing that rapid ascents often precipitate DCS, a diver arriv-

In the event a diver suffers from decompression sickness, a VHF radio is the fastest way to call for help. The Coast Guard monitors Channel 16 as do most boaters and harbormasters. In addition, local fishermen have their favorite working channels. It may be a significant help to contact them if you're far from shore.

ing at the surface from depth without a weight belt or without air, both suggesting a very rapid ascent, would be looked at as a very high risk candidate for DCS. Likewise, an examination of the diver's recent dive profile(s) may suggest no-decompression limits violations.

Decompression sickness may strike a diver in two forms categorized according to their severity and what parts of the body are affected. Type I may produce a rash-like reddening of the skin, usually on the upper body and arms. The affected areas are itchy and irritated, and may be accompanied by mild, transient joint pains (niggles). Taken together, skin itch and joint pains are a fairly accurate sign of DCS, especially if the history supports the possibility. Typically symptoms appear shortly after the dive, usually about 30 minutes, but onset may be delayed by 24 hours or more.

Joint pain is more common and often exists in the absence of skin involvement. Pressure from growing bubbles of nitrogen is thought to stimulate nerve transmission near affected joints, resulting in these fairly localized pains. Since these sensations are not related to strained or bruised muscles, or any other actual palpable injury, they are not readily affected by the application of hot or cold packs or even direct massage. The victim himself will describe these pains as deep and boring, rather than sharp.

If DCS is suspected, the rescuer should insist that the victim be taken to a diving physician at once. In this respect, the rescuer needs to be aware that

Carefully observe any diver who made a rapid ascent from depth. A diver who arrived at the surface out of air, without a weight belt or with a full BC may have ascended too rapidly. Decompression sickness may develop within 30 minutes of surfacing or may not become evident for 24-48 hours. Remember that the effects of DCS may progress from mild to severe over a very short period of time.

a high proportion of DCS victims will refuse to admit that their symptoms reflect a bends hit. Denial is a well-recognized aspect of early DCS onset. The victim may need to be coaxed with reason and calm persuasion to seek medical attention. Though Type I bends will likely pass on its own over time, there is no real method to predict that this will happen. Much more serious Type II bends could appear shortly and with it the risk of grave long-term injury. On-scene the rescuer should keep the victim calm, cool and relaxed. Energetic activity on the part of the victim will make the condition worse by hastening the release of nitrogen from solution, adding to the size and number of bubbles already in the tissues. Hot baths or showers serve the same purpose and should be avoided.

The rescuer should deliver high-flow O_2 to the victim for as long as possible during transport to a diving physician. Use of oxygen for treatment will often produce almost immediate relief for the victim. This merely confirms that the problem is DCS, but does not cure the patient. The definitive cure for DCS is recompression in a chamber. *TDI/SDI does not support in-water recompression as a safe practice for the field treatment of DCS.*

The more serious form of DCS, Type II bends, can be life-threatening to the victim and frightening to onlookers. Symptoms may cascade upon the victim in rapid succession, all of them debilitating and some of them bizarre. The source of the problem is growing nitrogen bubbles pressed hard against the spinal cord and even the brain. As such, any sign that demonstrates impairment of motor skills, thought processes, or behavior may strongly indicate Type II bends.

Signs and symptoms include staggering, transient or continuous numbness or paralysis of any part of the body, respiratory distress or choking, visual disturbances and pains. The senses are also affected, including touch, taste and hearing. Blotches of discolored skin may appear and disappear over the victim's body. There may be apparent weakness in limbs on one or both sides of the body. This bilateral appearance of weakness is distinctly different from the one-side only weakness often evident in a stroke victim or arterial gas embolism as discussed below.

Arrange for the immediate transport of a Type II bends victim to a diving physician. Follow the procedure outlined above for the field treatment of Type I bends during transport, but do not delay for any reason. Be prepared to administer CPR, if necessary, as respiratory paralysis is a real possibility in severe cases. Call for professional assistance as early as possible to meet with you and the victim en route to medical aid. Air transport via helicopter may be available in your area. Know how to contact the help you need.

Lung over-expansion injuries

The golden rule of scuba diving is never hold your breath while underwater. While the regulator sees to it that the air we breathe at any given depth is equal to the ambient pressure, changes in our depth will cause the air to expand or contract if we fail to exhale during this depth change. Holding our breath on ascent clearly holds more serious consequences as our lungs can only withstand a small amount of expansion beyond normal. The weakest links in the respiratory system are the alveoli, the tiny air sacs at the very end of the bronchiole tubes. Though elastic and flexible, the alveoli are delicate and have strict limits to expansion. It takes a rise of only a few feet in the water while holding your breath on compressed air for the alveoli to burst. Bubbles of air, escaping from the lung tissue, may travel to all parts of the body, with potentially life-threatening outcomes.

In reality it is not always necessary to breath-hold to cause this over-expansion to occur. Individuals with compromised respiratory systems and medical conditions, such bronchitis, emphysema, tuberculosis or those suffering from chest infections or colds, all possess lungs which have some existing blockage. In some cases this is temporary, but in others is a permanent feature. In either case, scuba diving is extremely hazardous to those persons as air may be trapped within partially obstructed alveoli and may not be able to escape before damaging expansion takes place.

Inadvertent breath-holding is another potential source of trouble. This happens every time we attempt to equalize pressures in our ears, or when an underwater photographer holds his breath to steady the camera, or when we use breathholding to stabilize our buoyancy. It also happens in an unexpected way when we stop for decompression in shallow water and the trough between swells passes overhead. There may be a drop of 4-5 ft. (1-1.5 m) in an instant when this occurs. What was a full breath as the swell passed over is now over-full when under the trough. For this reason it is frequently safer to hang from a line attached to a surface buoy or the boat, rather than one fixed and marked from the bottom.

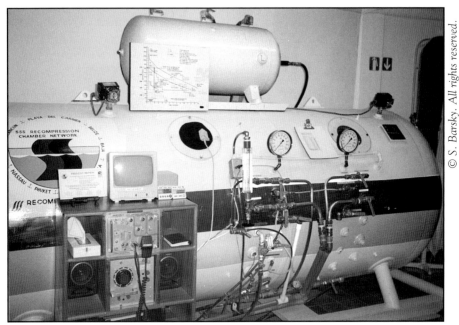

Decompression sickness and lung over-expansion injuries must be treated in a hyperbaric chamber.

Once air escapes from the alveoli and lung tissue, several outcomes are possible. Though we are not expected to make a specific diagnosis of which type of illness has resulted from the lung rupture, we need to be familiar with the range of signs we see and symptoms the victim tells us about to recognize that a lung rupture has taken place.

Mediastinal and subcutaneous emphysema

Emphysema describes a condition where air has gathered in and inflated some part of the body or an organ. Mediastinal refers to the center mid-point of the chest and includes the area containing the heart. Air escaping from the lung tissue may collect in this area and expand around the heart. This expansion may actually move the heart out of place and puts increased external pressure on it. The result may be a reduction in cardiac output and strain on the heart. As air continues to move freely around the thoracic cavity, it can rise along the trachea to come to rest under the skin, especially around the neck. This results in a bizarre condition, "subcutaneous emphysema," where the skin may crackle like cellophane paper, but has the more serious outcome of pressing on the victim's trachea. Breathing may become difficult as a result. While not grave emergencies in themselves, these conditions are, more importantly, indicators of a lung over-expansion and rupture.

What to look for:
1. Shortness of breath
2. Pain in the center of chest
3. Rapid, erratic pulse
4. Signs and symptoms of shock
5. Swelling around neck
6. Possible voice changes

What to do:
1. Recognize that a lung injury has occurred.
2. Support breathing efforts through O_2 therapy.
3. Be aware that you may be witnessing only the early stages of a progressively more serious sequence of events. Alert emergency medical personnel and transport as soon as possible.

Pneumothorax
The term pneumothorax describes a condition where air has escaped from the lungs and has crept between the pleural membranes that cover the lungs and the chest wall. These membranes serve as protective coatings on each, and also trap a lubricant between them to allow the lungs to slide along the chest wall with each inhalation and exhalation. As air flows between these membranes, and especially as it expands during the diver's continued ascent, the pleural membranes begin to strip away from each other. The expanding air also puts pressure on the lung and may cause it to collapse. At this point the lung, or the portion of it that has collapsed, is non-functional.

What to look for:
The diver will complain of pain, almost always on one side only, and may lean his body toward the injured side. Breaths will be labored and possibly painful. Other signs of respiratory distress such as coughing, wheezing, and cyanosis (blue tinge to the skin) may be evident. Notable in such cases is "tracheal shift." This is a condition where the lack of pressure in one lung

versus normal pressure in the other forces organs and the trachea toward the effected side.

Injured persons survive pneumothoraces every day, as there are many and varied causes for this injury. In the diving circumstance, however, the injured person is probably in the water, may have been unconscious, and possibly was without air for some period. The accident probably happened a long way from definitive medical care and the cause is a ruptured lung from expanding air.

What to do:

1. Recognize that a lung injury has occurred.
2. Respiratory dysfunction as indicated by breathing effort and cyanosis *always* requires that we support ventilations. Start the victim on O_2 as soon as possible.
3. Keep the patient comfortable and covered during transport to medical facilities.
4. Be aware that his condition may change for the worse. Be prepared to administer CPR.

Arterial gas embolism

The alveoli are the site of gas exchange in the body. This exchange takes place across the membrane of the alveoli and the walls of the capillaries which cover the surface of the alveoli. The capillaries carry blood loaded with CO_2 from the heart to the surface of the alveoli for the exchange to take place, and then carry the blood, now loaded with O_2, back to the heart for distribution throughout the body. When a lung rupture occurs, it's the alveoli that burst. When this happens, it's inevitable that capillaries surrounding the alveoli are torn as well.

In the most extreme case of a lung over-expansion injury, blood trickles into the alveoli and, even more ominous, air begins to enter the circulation through the open ends of these tiny blood vessels. The bubbles return to the heart and may then be pumped to all parts of the body. It happens, however, that the first major blood vessels that these bubbles encounter are the carotid arteries, the large vessels that feed directly into the brain.

As blood vessels enter an organ, whether the brain or even muscles, they divide in two. Each of these will divide in two, a process repeated many, many times. Eventually the smallest of blood vessels, capillaries, reach the point where they deliver their load of oxygen and begin to join together again.

Bubbles traveling this route will therefore enter progressively smaller vessels until they can no longer pass through the capillary. Blood flow in that vessel stops due to this blockage (embolism). Most critical is the fact that no tissue "down stream" of this point will receive oxygen, and the tissue begins to die. Since this embolism is caused by air and takes place on the arterial side of the circulation (as opposed to DCS-nitrogen bubbles on the venous side), this condition is referred to as arterial gas embolism or "AGE." Significantly, bubbles may not have to travel to the smallest vessels to become jammed. The bubbles may in fact be growing in size as the diver ascends, allowing for continued bubble growth after the air escapes into the circulation. Larger bubbles get trapped in larger vessels, meaning that greater areas of tissue become deprived of oxygen (ischemic). Note that the capillaries in the lungs will clot and seal themselves off very quickly after rupture. The damage is done early in the accident, though the consequences may follow up to 15 minutes later.

Thus, AGE is an immediately life-threatening condition where every second counts in recognition and taking the victim to definitive care. Even the chance that what you observe in a diver *might* be an air embolism necessitates activating the emergency medical system and arranging a hasty transport. All the lung-over-expansion injuries described above may appear in succession or even simultaneously. This makes for a stunning and frightening presentation to the observer. Keeping your *own* head and taking the correct steps may save a life, or a life-time of disability.

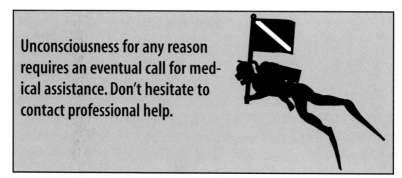

Unconsciousness for any reason requires an eventual call for medical assistance. Don't hesitate to contact professional help.

What to look for:

The onset of signs and symptoms of an arterial gas embolism may be sudden. The diver may collapse without warning after returning to the boat or may even arrive at the surface unconscious. The diver will show signs identical to a stroke, the cause in both cases is an embolism in the brain, bubbles in AGE or blood clot in stroke. Weakness on one side may be observed, the diver staggering and complaining of dizziness and severe head pain. Visual disturbances are common. Note that all other symptoms previously mentioned for lung over-expansion injuries may also be present.

What to do:
1. Recognize the likelihood of a lung over-expansion injury.
2. Recognize the possibility of AGE.
3. Lay the patient down on ground or deck of boat. He should not be made to walk anywhere.
4. Loosen tight clothing/exposure suit and treat for shock.
5. Deliver high-flow oxygen for as long as possible.
6. Transport as quickly as possible.
7. Be prepared to support life with CPR, until arriving at definitive medical care.

Marine life injuries:

It has often been said that the most dangerous and destructive animal in the ocean is a diver. Certainly it is generally true that we cause far more injury and upset to the wildlife through accident and harassment than it ever causes us. Still, opportunities exist for divers to come in contact with animals that are far from defenseless. Typically the victim is a novice diver who has yet to master good buoyancy control, or even an experienced diver new to the area. Local knowledge, good diving skills and a respect for the underwater environment will greatly lessen the chances of close encounters of the wrong kind.

Marine life injuries are classified according to the kind of wound caused rather than by the specific kind of animal involved.

There are many sharp spined fish like this east coast "sea raven." Most are drab, inconspicuous bottom dwellers that become more active at night.

Punctures- Includes bites and spine wounds

Sea urchin spines are hard, very brittle and often very sharp. Depending on the species, they vary in length from 1/4 to 8 inches (0.5-20 cm). They may easily break off under the skin on contact, and will certainly penetrate the average wet suit. Significant irritation and itching may result. A few tropical species inject a mild toxin.

Sculpins and related fish possess long, very sharp spines. The spines to beware of are typically the dorsal fin spines, though some species have an inconspicuous pectoral fin spine, as well. Most are quite sharp and strong, but breakage under the skin is fairly rare. Though usually quite painful if the puncture is deep, the major danger is infection rather than poison.

Other fish such as, lionfish, scorpionfish and stonefish possess highly toxic spines and are a distinct danger to divers. Lionfish spines are long (5-10"), thin and radiate from the dorsal and pectoral fins. From the front the fish seems to be surrounded by a halo of spines and is very striking in appearance. Stonefish spines are shorter and far less obvious. The fish itself is not very conspicuous and is very much like the northern sea raven in appearance, that is, squat, drab and well-camouflaged. Its spines, however, are no less poisonous than those of the lionfish.

Lionfish are docile, spectacular fish, but beware of their sharp, venomous spines.

Punctures from these spines produce an immediate intense pain that persists for many hours. The victim may show signs of weakness, nausea and vomiting. Cardiac arrest is possible.

Sting rays carry a sharp, barbed spine on their tails that is capable of inflicting a very painful wound. If molested, sting rays will defend themselves with this spine. Divers often encounter rays inadvertently while wading into the water. Shuffling your feet alerts the rays to the diver's approach and

Wolf fish have extremely powerful jaws and sharp teeth. Usually secretive and solitary, they are territorial and don't welcome close encounters.

allows the rays time to move away. This is an outstanding example of the best first aid being prevention.

Bites from marine animals are rare and almost always result from provoking the animal first. Any animal that is large enough to bite should be treated with caution. Be aware that some fish such as wolf fish and moray eels are highly territorial and have a very different view from humans as to what constitutes provocation. Larger predators (sharks and barracuda) may be dangerous in some circumstances and must always be treated with respect. Remember that although unprovoked attacks on divers underwater are vanishingly small, provocation is a relative term. Feeding sharks by hand may provide a diver with the thrill of a lifetime, but wild animals do not confine themselves to our rules. If it's capable of swimming away with your hand, maybe you shouldn't put your hand in its mouth.

What to do:

1. Clean wound thoroughly with fresh water and soap.

2. If spine particles are observed under the skin, these should be removed if possible. Left unattended and in place, these will become increasingly uncomfortable and result in infections over the next few weeks.

3. Non-poisonous bites may require control of bleeding as a priority. After bleeding is controlled and the wound cleaned, it should be covered with clean, dry bandages. Medical attention should be sought as the greatest danger remains infection.

4. Poisonous spine puncture may present a life-threatening emergency. The victim will be anxious and apprehensive, so calm and reassure him. As most wounds will be on the hands, feet and knees, the victim may need assistance in walking. The best on-scene treatment is immersion in hot water, basically as hot as the victim can tolerate. The spine toxin is heat-sensitive and can be denatured (broken down) by high heat. Be prepared to deal with airway obstructions due to vomiting and to give CPR, if necessary. Medical attention should be obtained as soon as possible.

Sea snake bites are fortunately rare, mainly because these reptiles are placid and not easily provoked. Even if bitten, there is an excellent chance that the diver will not be envenomated as many sea snakes are back-fanged. Fang punctures are, therefore, by no means assured. Nevertheless, seas snake venom is deadly and specific antivenin must be sought as soon as possible. Be sure to remember what the snake looked like so that the proper anti-venin can be selected. These reptiles do not occur in Atlantic or in Caribbean waters.

Symptoms of sea snake envenomation may not be obvious at first. The bite itself is not always painful and the effects start mildly. The victim becomes drowsy as the level of consciousness decreases. Swallowing and speaking become difficult. Complete paralysis with respiratory and cardiac arrest may follow.

What to do:

1.Poisonous sea snake bites are also life-threatening emergencies. The neurotoxic venom is powerful, but somewhat slow acting, so the first order of business is for everyone to stay *calm*. Increased activity on the part of the victim only speeds the circulation of the venom and the onset of more severe symptoms.

2. Clean the wound site thoroughly.

3. Apply a 2 inch (5 cm) wide constricting band, for example, a handkerchief, above and below the bite. These must *not* be too tight (you should be able to force your finger under the band). Loosen the bands for 1-2 minutes every hour.

4. Suctioning snake bit wounds is controversial and of dubious value in any case. You will probably better use the time to transport the victim to medical attention.

5. Splint the extremity to limit movement. Keep it below heart level.

6. Be prepared to assist ventilations, as necessary.

Many jellyfish have very long, nearly invisible tentacles and are capable of delivering potent stings.

Stings- Includes jellyfish and corals

Most jellyfish are graceful, harmless animals that are a delight to watch "swimming" underwater. A few species, however, are capable of delivering powerful, venomous stings to the bare skin of a diver. Specialized cells in the tentacles, called nematocysts, are really no more than spring-loaded harpoons that will fire their dart at any object that approaches too closely or touches the tentacle. Basically a food-gathering method, the impaled harpoon is reeled in complete with prey which is then raised into the body of the jellyfish. Even tentacles that have broken off from the main body of the jellyfish are still capable of stinging.

Symptoms of jellyfish envenomation may be severe and include:
- sharp, burning sensation
- inflammation
- nausea and fainting
- mental confusion and unconsciousness

Fire coral is the best known of the stinging corals. Soft, sponge-like, and an innocuous tan or brown color, fire coral contact on bare skin can produce an impressive reaction in a diver. The burning sensation is immediate and may progress to muscle and joint soreness. A few sensitive people may show more severe reactions. Fire coral is probably not highly dangerous (except in certain individuals), but accidentally kneeling on it can ruin your day.

What to do:

1. Wash skin carefully with warm water and soap to remove any clinging tentacles. Wear gloves to avoid contacting the tentacles directly.
2. Rinse skin with a dilute paste of baking soda or very dilute ammonia to help neutralize the acid-based venom. Some claim that vinegar works as well, but this is doubtful.
3. If the burning and itching persists, apply an antihistamine cream.
4. There may be severe generalized reactions that call for immediate medical attention. The patient may require respiratory and cardiac support during transport.

Note: There is considerable debate on the best way to prevent unfired nematocysts from discharging, if tentacles are still clinging to the skin. Some claim that vinegar poured over the tentacles will prevent this. Others claim that alcohol will "fix" the nematocysts and prevent their discharge. Finally, lab results have suggested that neither of these methods is effective on all species. Warm water, soap, gloves and quick response will probably serve you as well as anything else and with much less fuss.

Jellyfish tentacles can sting even after they've broken off the main part of the body. The nematocysts can sting as long as they are wet.

Cuts and Scrapes

By far the most common injuries to divers while diving will be cuts and scrapes from bumping into or rubbing against abrasive objects. Typical examples are knee or elbow scrapes from coral outcrops, and hand and knee cuts from barnacles. Poor buoyancy control and simple inattention are the usual culprits here, though experience with these mishaps serves as a notable memory prod to be careful where you put your hands in the future. With the exception of fire coral already discussed, coral and barnacles are neither poi-

sonous nor menacing. They can, however, be as sharp as a razor and effort-
lessly lacerate water-softened skin. These cuts often run deep and can be
quite painful. Even worse, left attended, they will often become infected and
cause intense irritation for many days.

The infection risk comes from the fact that the edges of the coral or barnacle are far from clean, and the deep cuts introduce all manner of infectious
agents under the skin. Unless the wound site is carefully cleaned and disin-
fected, some discomfort down the road is a sure bet.

What to do:

1. Wash the cuts and abrasions carefully with warm water and soap.
2. Rinse thoroughly with fresh water, making sure that the cuts
themselves are flushed out.
3. Paint the area with a Betadine-type (iodine) solution or spread on
an antibiotic cream.
4. Small wounds dry and heal better if left open, but larger scrapes
may ooze and will need to be covered with an absorbent bandage.

Scuba I.Q. Review

1. What indicators of problems that your buddy may be experiencing might be apparent to you?
2. What are the watchwords to keep in mind in any underwater problem?
3. Describe the carotid sinus reflex.
4. What is the danger of carbon monoxide contamination in a diver's air supply?
5. What is the best way to deal with nitrogen narcosis problems?
6. Describe the physics of an ear squeeze.
7. Why is the BC a factor in dry suit squeezes?
8. What is a barotrauma?
9. Why is recommended ascent rate only 30 ft. (9 m) per minute?
10. List some contributing factors to the occurrence of decompression sickness.
11. What is the difference between Type I and Type II bends?
12. What is the on-scene treatment of choice in the event of decompression sickness?
13. How does a lung over-expansion injury happen?
14. List the most common signs and symptoms of a lung over-expansion injury.
15. Why is a lung over-expansion injury immediately life threatening?
16. Why is decompression sickness a venous gas embolism and bubbles in the blood from a lung over-expansion injury an arterial gas embolism?
17. Describe the signs and symptoms of a venomous puncture wound from a lionfish or stonefish.
18. Describe how you would handle the tentacles of a stinging jellyfish.

Chapter 6
Dive Accident
Management

Dive Site Organization

Whether diving from a luxurious live-aboard dive boat or from one of our spectacular rocky shorelines, all divers will obviously benefit from a well-run operation. One advantage of organization is the security of knowing that all support persons are practiced and rehearsed in their roles. The other benefit is not always obvious... until there is an accident on the dive scene.

A well-run dive boat will have someone assigned to assist divers from the water, helping avoid over-exertion and possible injury.

Chapter 6
Personnel

A busy, well-run dive site will be under the supervision of personnel who take their roles seriously. There may be instructors present, but for the most part non-training dives are conducted by the divemasters. Even on training dives, a divemaster on scene often functions as a foreman, keeping things on schedule, ensuring divers are briefed on the underwater features and hazards, and serving as the point person in a trouble-shooting role. Depending on the kinds of diving being undertaken, there may be safety divers available, extra hands to assist divers in and out of the water, and the dive recorder. Dive accidents on a well-planned, well-run dive site are especially rare, but can happen anywhere. This is where the great "silent" benefit of a good organizational plan becomes clear.

A dive crew should be able to fall instantly into their new roles in managing the accident with the view to mitigating a potential injurious situation, and helping keep it from getting worse. Having an accustomed station in the event of a diving emergency gives the crew, which might well include certified rescue divers, a blueprint for action.

Among those who will be called to respond to the scene will be highly trained professionals who may be able to assist or even take the lead in managing the incident. Such teams, often associated with Public Safety departments have very specialized skills and abilities, as well as specific local knowledge. They will likely also have the kinds of equipment that even a well-organized dive center might not have. *Never hesitate to call for assistance if you think it could be helpful. Emergency response teams do this kind of thing for a living, and can be formidable assets in a crisis.*

A planned response to a diving incident is similar to fire drill rehearsals in schools; it prepares us for the unthinkable, and helps to avoid time wasted in wondering what to do next (or first!). The dive leader may send out the recall signal to bring all divers back, task rescue divers to assist a victim in the water, assign someone to begin recording the events and times of occurrence and someone else to summon more help to the scene.

Rescue divers understand their role, as well, having been trained in dealing with the desperate injuries that can occur in a hyperbaric environment. Others on board or on the shore know how to contact and activate emergency medical services (EMS). A planned and practiced response, as well as appointed roles and the relevant contact information may be as important to the survival of a victim as the skills and speed of response of professional assistance.

Accident scene behavior
• Be gentle with people.
• Preserve the victim's dignity
• Stay calm yourself
• Be reassuring in a crisis situation

The Emergency Plan

Tending an injured diver is not always a straightforward procedure. The injured person may be a friend of yours, maybe even your buddy. Often there are family members present on the site. There are complex emotional issues in these cases. There will be fear, confusion and much anxiety. Professionals try to remove distractions from the scene, as much to help them keep a clear head as to "give the victim room to breathe". Here are a few rules professional rescuers use:

- Never forget the dignity of the person you're assisting.
- Avoid making a fuss of minor incidents, i.e., don't cause him undue embarrassment.
- Do not talk about him in the third person in front of others. Use his name.
- Do not shriek in alarm at the sight of the victim's blood or other injuries. Even an unconscious person often hears every word that is said.
- *Reassure* the victim. Mental state is *very* important to survival.
- The rescuer's attitude is solicitous, never condescending.

Recognize

The first step in assisting a diver in distress is recognition of an emergency. The principle features and signs of a diver in trouble have been reviewed in Chapters 3 & 4. One common cause for delay on any accident scene, however, is a persistent reluctance to commit to action. This is frequently observed in persons who have no prior training in accident recognition and conditioned response. Bystanders watch passively while someone is injured or attacked. The mind simply refuses to believe what it is witnessing. Even trained lifeguards will sometimes hesitate before responding to a swimmer in trouble. The possibility of embarrassment to the rescuer caused by an all-out response to a situation that has been misinterpreted or where the res-

Breaking waves are just one way divers may receive injuries through inattention.

cuer may fail in front of onlookers can root the rescuer to the spot. Remember that for every second you debate the pros and cons of action, a second is lost. Don't fail through inaction.

Respond

Response options depend in great measure on the type of incident in progress. On an organized scene, a dive leader may take charge and direct others to the best advantage of the victim. If you are rescue qualified, you may become an invaluable and integral part of any response. In a small group you may well be the most highly qualified person on scene. Your assessment and judgment will become paramount in any response taken. Specific response options for many categories of diver distress have already been detailed in earlier chapters, however, there may be much more to do as well. Other participants should be assigned to provide specific assistance.

Preparation before the dive will have included contact telephone numbers for EMS and rescue personnel. These may be provided by local police, fire or ambulance services. At sea or in navigable waters, the Coast Guard or harbor patrols will always be a first option for aid. Although most often the first communications with Coast Guard stations will be via marine VHF radio, further communications are often easier and more secure via cell

Whenever possible, assign other persons on scene to assist in the recovery of the injured diver. This may be especially important during the removal of the diver from the water.

phone. The U.S. Coast Guard monitors channel 16, but once contact is established you will likely be requested to switch to another working frequency. When on the radio, keep your communications short and concise. Be able to tell other boaters or responding rescue vessels exactly where you are. Learn the local landmarks and always note the position (latitude and longitude) of the dive vessel.

Any rescue equipment on board the vessel should be readied. This might include throwing devices, extra PFDs, a backboard, first aid kit and oxygen kit. You may be the only person on the dive scene who can give the correct first aid and administer oxygen, but it helps if others can ready this essential equipment. Recall any other divers from the water. In a real emergency, it becomes extremely difficult to keep track of people. Use other divers to assist you if this is within their capability, but don't endanger anyone else. Their most effective role may be to assist in the removal of the victim from the water after you have recovered and towed him back to the boat/shore.

Rescue

Circumstances that require you to enter the water to assist another diver will always put you at some risk. Do not overlook the hazards to you in choosing to respond. Water rescue can be a dangerous business; you must be cer-

A diver using a signal device to get attention may be calling for immediate assistance.

tain of your abilities and level of fitness before you commit to an in-water rescue.

Whenever possible, enlist the assistance of other qualified individuals to make the job easier. This may include help in towing a person to the boat/shore, someone holding a paddleboard or other flotation device, help in removing the victim from the water, a bystander sent to alert the nearest Emergency Medical Services station, or even to fetch appropriate equipment for on-scene treatment. Be careful not to press persons without good water skills or presence of mind into stressful situations. Nearby lifeguards, harbor

The 4Rs Emergency Plan
- **Recognize that a person is in danger.**
- **Respond in a practiced, appropriate manner.**
- **Rescue and return the victim to safety.**
- **Record all events, victim information and treatment delivered.**

patrol officers and harbormasters are often good sources of hands-on help. Despite all this, never forget the golden rule of rescue; *you are the most important person on the rescue scene*. When rescuers forget that, we too often end up with one more victim and one less rescuer. Your own safety is always your most important responsibility.

Record

In the aftermath of the flurry of activity that accompanies an actual in-water rescue, especially of an injured scuba diver, participants typically experience only vague memories of the sequence of events. Stories are confused and contradictory, and it seems that no one paid any attention to the time. It's important to delegate the responsibility of record keeping early to someone on scene. There are several reasons for this. In the event of a missing diver, it may be critical to know just how long the victim may have been submerged. A diver last seen on the surface will likely have drifted. Knowing the set and drift of the current will aid searchers who will be looking for the victim, *if* they know when he was last seen. Also, a good working record of the rescuer/dive leaders' responses will aid in the reconstruction of the incident.

Finally, it's important to log all of your efforts in reviving, treating and transporting the victim to safety. These records are an invaluable part of the patient records that should accompany the victim to the medical authorities. This will help medical personnel evaluate the effectiveness of on-scene treatment and give them a good clue as to the patient's progress. Your data are the baseline from which all further examinations are measured. Do not underestimate the value of your initial surveys of respiratory rate, heart rate and the other features of importance in these early surveys.

Assessing the diver's injuries

Most diver injuries are minor. Events that result in sprained ankles and cut fingers are easy to see and diagnose. Occasions when a diver may complain of vague headaches or dizziness, or inexplicable tiredness, or any changes in his level of consciousness should raise a red flag for the rescue diver. Certainly, any diver who experienced even a brief period of unconsciousness will be a cause for concern and further investigation. The best approach to assessing injuries is a systematic one that falls into the "primary survey" and the "secondary survey."

Remove the diver's hood to check for the carotid artery pulse.

The scene survey

This quick review of the scene is safety-oriented with the identification of dangers to the victim and rescuer the principle object. Is there continuing danger to the victim if left in place? Would it be best to move the victim to another place? Are there any dangers to the rescuers in operating here? Is time a factor?

The primary survey

This consists of the A, B, C's, for airway, breathing and circulation.

Airway- Check to determine if the victim's airway is clear.

    Can the victim speak?

    Is there any danger of obstruction such as bitten-off pieces of mouthpieces or vomitus?

Breathing- Check to determine if the victim is breathing.

    Look for rise and fall of the chest.

    Listen for breath sounds.

    Feel exhaled breath on your cheek.

Circulation- Check to determine that the victim has a pulse.
Feel for a pulse at the carotid artery in the neck. Victim's hood must be removed.

If no breath sounds can be determined, then rescue breathing must begin before checking for circulation.

Rescue Breathing

• Begin by tilting the victim's head back by lifting the chin and opening the mouth. Ensure that no blockage is evident. If any is observed, use a finger sweep to retrieve and clear the articles.

• Seal your mouth over the victim's mouth, pinch his nose closed and exhale two full breaths into the victim. Use of a pocket mask will provide you with protection from the transmission of diseases possible with direct mouth-to-mouth resuscitation.

• If the chest does not rise with your attempted exhalations into the victim's lungs, or if you feel total resistance to these breaths, the airway may be blocked farther down. Try repositioning the head and inflating the lungs again.

• Failure to inflate the lungs after repositioning the head, implies a blockage.

For a victim supine on the deck or ground, straddle the victim's legs and place one hand on top of the other on the victim's abdomen. Thrust hard with your hands into the abdomen and towards the victim's chest along the midline of the body. The effect should be to push the diaphragm upward as in a hard exhalation to clear the obstruction in the airway. Repeat this several times and check the mouth for the obstruction. Attempt another breath. If the airway is still blocked, repeat the procedure. Until the airway can be cleared, there may be little else we can do to help the victim.

Once breaths can be successfully delivered to the non-breathing victim, the next step is to check for a pulse. If the diver is wearing a hood, this must be carefully removed to find the carotid artery. Most often it is quicker and easier on the victim if you simply cut the hood off. This is best done using blunt-point shears. Start the cut at an edge nearest the victim's mouth or chin, and continue toward the neck and collar. The hood will loosen as you cut and get easier. Take no more than 5 seconds to do this.

Palpate (feel) for the pulse for about 5-10 seconds using your fingers (not your thumb which has a measurable pulse of its own). Failure to find a pulse indicates that the victim's heart has stopped. We can aid the victim by external cardiac compressions which simulate a beating heart. To be effective, we need to open the zipper of any wet suit jacket the victim may be wearing. It will not be necessary at this stage to remove the jacket.

- Position yourself alongside the supine victim at about mid-chest level.
- Trace the edge of the rib cage back to the "V" of the sternum (breastbone).
- Measure a 3-finger-width distance mark toward the neck from the "V."
- At this mark place the heel of one hand, then stack your other hand on top.
- Lean your upper body over your hands and push sharply in to the victim's chest. Compress the chest about 2" and release.

CPR requires both cardiac compression and rescue breathing. As a solo rescuer we need to keep a regular rhythm that alternates between compressions and breaths.

Dive site treatment includes a thorough primary and secondary survey,

One Person CPR-
- Start with two full initiating breaths.
- Immediately find your mark and do 15 full compressions at the rate of about 80-100 per minute.
- Immediately give another two breaths and return to compressions.
- After about a minute of compressions and breaths, or 4 full cycles, stop and look again for a pulse. Take ten seconds for this as before. The first minute cycle of breaths and compressions may have restarted the heart and breathing cycles. If not, begin CPR again. Stop and check for a pulse and natural breathing every few minutes.

TDI/SDI recommends that all divers learn and be certified to perform effective CPR and be trained to deliver oxygen at the scene of a diving accident. The TDI/SDI CPROX and CPR-First programs are a good example of this essential training. Your diving instructor will be able to give you specific information on this valuable course.

The secondary survey

If the patient is breathing and has a pulse, the rescuer will conduct the secondary survey. This is a head to toe examination with the intention of finding any other injuries to the victim.

Check and record vital signs and level of conscious for changes every 15 minutes. These changes are the best indicators that a patient is improving or deteriorating.

Vital Signs
- Respirations- Check and record.
   - Normal is between 10-20 per minute and effortless.
- Heart rate- Check and record.
   - Normal is 50-90 beats per minute and steady.
- Check and record skin color, temperature and moisture.
   - Skin- check characteristics
   - Color- skin, nail beds, eyelids should be pink.
   - Temperature- warm
   - Moisture- dry, but is obviously an uncertain indicator in divers.

Level of Consciousness
- Alert and oriented- fully conscious and aware of surroundings.
- Responds to verbal stimuli- Answers questions, though may be confused.

Responds to painful stimuli- Cannot speak, but responds to pinching. Unresponsive- Will not respond to any stimuli, fully unconscious.

Patient Examination
• Start at the head. Gently slide your hands under the back of the victim's head to feel for blood, bumps or deformities. Slide hands under back of neck to ensure proper alignment, absence of blood and deformities. Check for blood or other fluids in ears, nose and mouth.

•Slide hands over chest and gently press. Check for bruising or blood and any unevenness. Run hands over abdomen. Stomach muscles should be relaxed and normal. Stomach muscles held rigid may indicate internal injury to organs, and possible internal bleeding.

• Continue examination over legs and arms. If conscious, have the patient confirm sensation in extremities.

Does the patient react to any of these contacts? Is there pain associated with any area? Is the dive suit torn or scuffed anywhere? Can the victim relate the history of the accident? Were there witnesses? Can you deduce what may have happened from the circumstances and examination of the diver's equipment?

Diving accidents include several circumstances that may lead to injuries to the brain or other parts of the nervous system. These include any temporary period without oxygen such as near-drowning, other non-breathing unconsciousness situations, bubbles of air or nitrogen in the brain or nervous system, or being struck in the head by a boat. It is imperative that we conduct an examination on any diver we suspect might be suffering from such an injury as soon as possible. This examination is directed specifically to those functions that are under the control of the brain or central nervous system. We're testing neurological function in this case, so this process is called a "neurological exam," or "neuro exam."

Neurological examination

The examination should be conducted with the patient "in from the weather" if the patient shows signs of distress. The first examination should be conducted as soon as possible after the onset of the first symptoms, and repeated every 15 minutes afterwards for at least the first hour.

Oxygen therapy may be the most important treatment you can deliver at the accident scene. A non-rebreather mask delivers upwards of 90% oxygen to the victim.

Orientation

Does the diver know his name and age? Does he know where he is? Is he oriented to time? These simple questions are important as they may reveal confusion in an impaired diver.

Muscle strength

Bear down on the diver's shoulders while he shrugs. Is strength approximately equal on both sides? Check arm strength by having diver resist your effort to raise or lower his arms.

Balance and coordination

Ask the diver to stand with eyes closed and raise arms out to the sides. From this position, then have the diver bring hands together, palm to palm, in front of body.

Eyes

Are the diver's pupils equal and reactive? Can the patient identify distant objects? Can the patient correctly count the number of fingers you hold in front of his face equally well with both eyes?

Sensory

With the patient's eyes closed, gently touch the patient's skin and scalp (ask first!) with your finger tips to ensure equal detection of sensations on both sides of the body.

Swallowing reflex

Instruct the patient to swallow while you watch the movement of the "Adam's apple." Look for a regular up and down motion, as well as that it has not been displaced to one side.

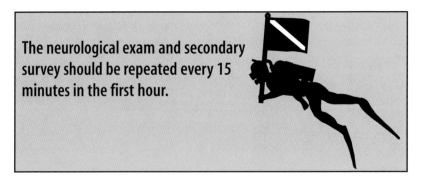

The neurological exam and secondary survey should be repeated every 15 minutes in the first hour.

Shock

One of the more serious consequences of injury may be shock. Because of the urgency it imparts to the accident scene, it's important to understand just what it is and how it works. Shock is normally brought about because of a radical drop in the body's fluid level. For this reason it is referred to most often as "hypovolemic shock."

Whenever an injury results in considerable bleeding, whether internal or external, or loss of fluid through profuse sweating and vomiting, then the circulatory system is unable to transport sufficient blood, and thus oxygen, to all parts of the body. The brain then switches circulation away from the other tissues and directs it only to itself, the heart and the lungs. This cannot continue indefinitely, however, without irreversible harm being done to the body and eventually the brain itself. Therefore, *shock is a life-threatening emergency and must receive immediate attention.*

What to look for:
- Victim appears restless and apprehensive
- Breathing is light and rapid
- Pulse is rapid and may feel "thin"
- Patient's skin is pale, cool, and clammy
- May be unsteady and staggering

- May vomit
- Diminishing level of consciousness
- May collapse suddenly

A good or even suggestive history can help. Since we are assuming that shock is the result of a diving injury, we will likely see shock as a consequence of those accidents that may produce a hypovolemic state. Examples of shock-producing dive injuries include, <u>external</u> <u>blood</u> <u>loss</u> from arterial bleeding from cuts or large fish bite, <u>internal</u> <u>blood</u> <u>loss</u> from lung over-expansion injuries or blunt trauma to the body, e.g., being struck in the torso by a tending boat, or <u>dehydration</u> from profuse sweating or vomiting.

What to do:
1. Calm and reassure the patient.
2. Determine and treat the cause of the shock reaction.
3. Victim should be placed on his back with the feet slightly elevated.
4. Remove wet suit hood and loosen suit.
5. Monitor vitals closely.
6. Maintain an open airway and watch for vomiting.
7. Give oxygen and get help.

Shock may be immediately life threatening.

On-scene oxygen therapy

It is clear that one of the most significant first aid remedies that rescuers can apply in a diving emergency is supplying oxygen to the victim. Oxygen may diminish the size of nitrogen bubbles in DCS, easing pains and limiting long-term tissue damage. It can also reduce the size of air bubbles in AGE, as well as help preserve tissue cut off from direct blood flow. In fact, any time we have reason to believe that either the respiratory or circulatory systems may be compromised, we should deliver oxygen to the patient. TDI/SDI

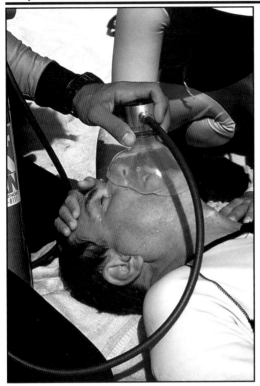

A demand valve oxygen regulator delivers the highest percentage of pure gas and has the added advantage of wasting the least amount of oxygen through spillage. This is not only more efficient, giving longer delivery times, but is safer as it reduces the chance of oxygen-induced combustion.

CPROX training will help you to determine what type of kit, size of cylinders, and what array of masks you might use, given the nature of your typical diving activities. Consideration of how far you might have to transport a diving accident victim to a medical facility will also dictate how much oxygen you should have on scene.

In general, you should have as much oxygen on hand as you can reasonably carry. Oxygen cylinders are sized by the number of liters of gas they contain. As with scuba cylinders, they are available both in steel and aluminum construction. For our purposes, we will probably want to provide oxygen for at least 30 minutes during the initial assessment and transport. We will almost certainly want to deliver oxygen at as high a rate (in liters per minute or LPM) as possible. Flow rates below 10 LPM would be selected in cases where the patient is conscious, resting and breathing comfortably. The typical setting on a O_2 regulator in this case would be 6 LPM. For a patient experiencing greater respiratory or circulatory distress, we would select a higher setting, typically around 10-15 LPM. The cylinder size, and therefore the amount of oxygen required, will determine how long we will be able to continue to provide oxygen to the patient.

It follows, then, that to be effective in providing the most satisfactory supply of oxygen to the patient at the flow rates discussed above, we should use a cylinder or cylinders with at least 300-450 liters capacity. Cylinders designated "D" or "E" ,and the so-called jumbo "D," contain between 350 and 625 liters and would be appropriate for a dive scene. For oxygen delivery in the lower ranges the patient may be fitted with a nasal cannula. This arrangement uses tubes to delivery oxygen to the patient's nostrils and has the advantage of not blocking the mouth or face. The victim can talk and is easy to monitor. It also does not interfere with airway control in the event the victim vomits. The downside is that the patient only receives about 30-40% oxygen, and much oxygen is wasted through spillage between breaths.

For more serious cases where high percentages of O_2 are required, a standard non-rebreather mask with reservoir bag is essential. This should be used with a high flow setting (10-15 LPM). Oxygen concentrations of 90% can be provided to the patient in this configuration. Oxygen delivery systems that employ a demand-type regulator, similar in many respects to a scuba regulator, also deliver very high concentrations of oxygen to the patient. There is an added advantage in that O_2 flows only on demand, thus decreases the amount spilled through the free-flow style of mask. *Rarely will we provide O_2 to a diving accident victim at anything but the highest percentages we can achieve.*

Protect the victim's head, neck, and aiway during transport and removal from the water.

Hypothermia Treatment

Prolonged exposure to environmental conditions that result in a net heat loss will eventually lead to hypothermia. While the exposure time varies with temperature and amount of environmental protection the diver has, until we remove the diver from the environment, we cannot fight the effects of cold injury. In warm climates, it may be enough to simply remove the diver from the water for them to rewarm naturally, though it will probably be helpful to keep the effect of wind-chill to a minimum by covering them with a blanket. In cooler conditions we may need to move chilled divers to a more sheltered area. This may be below decks on a larger boat or in a vehicle for shore-based dives. Depending on the extent of compromise due to hypothermia and how remote the dive site is from an actual, indoor warm area, we may have to take more action than that.

A diver suffering from moderate hypothermia will be shivering violently, be somewhat cyanotic, may slur his speech, have difficulty walking and will appear weak. Even out of the water the diver may continue to cool due to wind exposure and evaporative heat loss, unless we can bring him in from the weather. Lacking immediate access to a warm shelter, stabilize the victim by using some version of a "hypothermia wrap." Essentially, a hypothermia wrap is a windproof, waterproof covering within which we'll enfold the diver. Though commercial models, such as the "Brr...ito" are available, homemade versions consist of a tarp, a wool blanket and a reflective metal-film blanket.

In practice, the tarp is spread on the ground, the reflective blanket laid on the tarp, and the wool blanket laid on top of that. In northern areas, many divers and water rescuers carry the whole thing rolled up like a sleeping bag and stored in a plastic garbage bag in case of emergency. It's a good addition on board a dive boat, as well.

Removing the patient's exposure suit outdoors in extreme weather may be a mistake. If the air temperature is very cold, it's perfectly acceptable to wrap the victim, suit and all, in the hypothermia wrap. If conscious, give the patient warm, sweetened fluids to drink. These need not be hot as the warmth these drinks impart is more psychological than of any real physiological value. Ideally, rewarming should be *gradual* and by heat generated from within the victim's body. We can aid this by permitting the cold diver some *mild* activity such as walking, after which we'll wrap the victim again to prevent heat loss. Oxygen is indicated if the diver remains cyanotic or shows respiratory distress.

Never immerse a hypothermic victim in hot water. This may induce a condition known as "after-drop" which may cause a person to go into cardiac arrest.

• Temperature extremes in any direction will affect a diver's performance.
• Stay alert to the effects of hypothermia and hyperthermia.
• Fluids and oxygen are appropriate in both cases.

Hyperthermia Treatment

Unless cooled through immersion in cool water, a diver can rapidly and dangerously over-heat in an exposure suit. Muscle cramps may be the first sign of over-heating, though dizziness and an overwhelming tiredness may weaken the diver as he demonstrates the early stages of heat exhaustion. The diver will be *pale and sweating* profusely in an desperate attempt to cool himself and will be beginning to suffer from fluid loss as a result. *Do not ignore the diver who complains of the heat and who is showing its effects.* Cool the diver by stripping off the exposure suit or allowing him in the water to cool. Give him plenty of cool, clear fluids to drink to prevent dehydration. Sport drinks are also useful for electrolyte replacement.

Left unattended, heat exhaustion may rapidly progress to heat stroke, a true life-threatening emergency. Heat stroke is, in fact, the second leading cause of athletic death after head injury. Speed of recognition and response is critical to preventing permanent brain injury or death of the victim. The victim will be listless, possibly unresponsive, with a rapid, stronger than normal pulse (bounding), rapid breathing and the skin will be *hot, red and dry*.

Immediately cool the diver as rapidly as possible by dousing with cold water, ice (if available), and loosen all clothing. The brain can easily be damaged by the body's internal temperature (upwards of 105ºF or 40ºC by this stage), so pay particular attention to cooling the head. If conscious, the patient should be given as much fluid to drink as possible. Be alert to the possibility of vomiting, however, and be prepared to keep the victim's airway unobstructed. Among other things, he will be suffering from hypovolemic (low fluid level) shock. If oxygen is available, it should be provided to the diver at high flow rates. Advanced medical treatment will likely be required. Do not delay in getting help.

A simple precaution such as a suspended tank with regulator in place can help divers in low-air situations, and allow decompressing divers full, required stop time before surfacing.

Scuba I.Q. Review

1. Why is good, general dive site organization a benefit in the event of a diving accident?

2. List and explain the four R's of the emergency plan.

3. Who is the most important person on the accident scene?

4. What is meant by the A, B, C's of the primary survey?

5. What are the indications that CPR should be begun on a diving accident victim?

6. What will we measure and record on the Secondary Survey?

7. Describe the steps in a field neurological examination.

8. How often should the secondary survey and neuro exam be repeated?

9. What is shock and how do we treat it?

10. Why is oxygen therapy so valuable in treating diving injuries?

11. List and describe the main methods of delivering oxygen to the patient.

12. How do we recognize hypothermia?

13. What are the signs and symptoms of heat exhaustion and heat stroke?

Notes:

Chapter 7
Lost Diver Search and Recovery

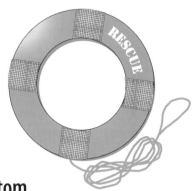

Searching for a diver on the bottom

Despite our best efforts, it sometimes happens that divers become separated underwater. Differences in interests cause some divers to slow down to look at tiny, attached marine life, while others swim on ahead looking for that elusive wreck. Photographers frequently stop to get a close up of some item of interest, or to wander off, practices well-known to drive dive buddies to distraction.

Failure to keep good buddy contact over long swims also accounts for separation of divers. The best buddy pairs or groups allow for the slower swimmers to set the pace. Whatever the reason, it happens frequently enough that divers perform the "lost buddy search" numerous times in their diving careers (see Chapter 1). Though a frustrating inconvenience, if all divers follow the

Pay particular attention to a diver who surfaces alone. It may indicate an uncontrolled ascent alone, an out-of-air emergency, a dropped weight belt, or the result of a lost buddy search.

same procedure, then they are always reunited on the surface within the next couple of minutes.

Still, it can, and does, happen that the divers are separated because one of them has had a serious problem, or develops such a problem after separation. The lost diver has become a missing diver. In previous chapters we've seen many ways in which divers can get into trouble on the surface and underwater. In the event that a diver is missing and unaccounted for 10 minutes, we have to assume that there has been a problem that is keeping him from surfacing. At this point we will likely make the decision that we have to find him.

Organizing the search

Relying on blind luck is rarely the most successful means of finding a lost person underwater. A thought-out and planned search will, over the long run, almost invariably produce more consistent results and should always be our first response to a missing diver emergency. Nevertheless, there are some occasions when a random search may be the better choice. These situations will be discussed later.

Last Known Point

The most important piece of early information we can acquire is a good sense of the missing diver's last known point. This information may come from the diver's buddy who might have a very good idea of where the separation occurred. The diver should at least know where the separation was first noticed which is as good a starting point as any.

Shore or boat observers may be the source of last known point information as well. Alert observers tend to watch the divers' bubbles as a matter of course and generally can determine an approximate area to search. Also, the point where the buddy surfaced is a valuable clue. If the surfacing buddy followed the general rules for a lost buddy search, then he'll likely not be far from the last known point. Finally, the missing diver may have surfaced at some time and gone back down again. This may have been a deliberate attempt to locate his buddy or may have been to an overweighting problem or other factors. Observers, seeing a lone diver on the surface, would have noticed this event and mentally recorded it.

We might have a choice of last known points or we may have none. If there are candidates for possible search locations, these should be marked with buoys for immediate investigation. Otherwise, we will need to try to reconstruct the activities of the divers from the buddy's narrative, and devise a defined search-area with a suitable search plan.

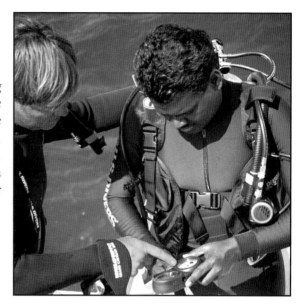

Interviewing the missing diver's buddy should provide us with information on the circumstances of the dive, how deep they were diving, how long they had been in the water and how much air the lost diver had left.

Available personnel

The worst of all possibilities is that you are the only diver on scene and that the missing diver is your buddy. Under these circumstances, you may be the worst of all choices to be the search diver. You are probably tired, low on air, maybe getting cold and probably carrying a burden of great apprehension and guilt. In terms of diving preparedness and mental preparation, you are not the ideal candidate for the solo diving required to conduct a safe and thorough search. *After determining some landmarks and being assured that you can located this exact spot again, leave the water, if necessary, and get help.*

If there are other people on the dive site, shout to get their attention and let them know what the nature of the emergency is. Divers on neighboring boats or farther down the beach can be recruited to assist in the search. In addition many public safety departments have dive teams who may be able to respond to the area quickly. Although persons who have drowned have been resuscitated after as much as an hour of submergence, these are very rare cases. The more divers we can mobilize to the scene, the more likely we can recover the lost person in the shortest time.

Any dive scene with multiple divers underwater simultaneously requires organization, and the search scene more than most. It's critical to everyone's safety that someone has an overview of the situation and is not actively diving. This person, who may be a divemaster or rescue diver, will determine

Be sure of your own navigational abilities before you undertake any underwater searches.

specific areas and search patterns for the divers to cover. Any divers participating in the search must first be cleared for diving in this endeavor. While we may not be able to prohibit unqualified divers from participating, we need to exercise some control over who dives where. In terms of search coverage, this is important. More importantly, however, is not allowing persons to dive beyond their training and experience.

Depth of water, currents, visibility and many other factors may pose significant challenges to less experienced divers. These challenges will become hazards in the high stress conditions of search. Moreover, divers responding from other dive sites, for example, other boats or shore sites, will probably be carrying their own burden of nitrogen from previous dives. They may have limited air and be tired. Like you, as the missing diver's buddy, they may be poor choices to search an unknown bottom under stress. Still, someone must dive. Choose carefully to avoid placing others in danger.

With all this in mind, the arrival on scene of an independent, fresh group of divers in a Public Safety team can be a real blessing. They will have their own organization, practiced techniques and available backup. It is best to allow them to take the lead in the search, though most groups will welcome your information and continued diving activities. Referring to the marker buoys you've placed that indicate areas already searched, and providing them with all the information you have, will help greatly in narrowing the search parameters to find the missing diver sooner.

Search Planning
- Gather as much information as possible.
- Define the major search area.
- Divide the major area into easily searched portions.
- Designate a well-marked starting point.
- Determine a stop point in advance.
- All search divers/dive teams must be tended or observed.

Good dive site organization will show itself in rapid assignment of roles for a search and rescue operation.

Carefully review the parameters for your part of the search effort before you and your buddy submerge.

Search Plans

There are many good search plans available for divers to employ when looking for a lost diver underwater. Most of them, however, require practice to conduct effectively. Besides, these practice sessions will have best been conducted under controlled conditions, not under the exigencies of a real rescue. For a complete review of search techniques, the reader should refer to texts that deal in this topic as a specialization. For the rescue diver, there are still a couple of good, simple search patterns that are both effective and straightforward. All search and rescue techniques, however, should be practiced to be effective.

Search areas need to be made manageable in size so that divers are not sent out to inspect seemingly endless expanses of bottom. Each specific area needs to have clearly defined boundaries, a designated start point and a designated stop point. Usually it's best if these points are pre-set and marked in advance. This way the divers know when they've finished an area and can rest, move to the next area, or search the same area again. Markers should be left for future reference to indicate areas that have been searched.

Search and rescue diver preparing for night operations. Note pony bottle and spare mask tucked in BC pocket.

Circular search

The circular search is very simple to perform, can be done by a single diver, and is still amongst the most effective of all searches in open water. In principle, the diver swims around a fixed point, attached to the point by a tether line. After completing one revolution, the diver may move away from the point by a measured distance of line, determined by underwater visibility and other factors, and will then swim another revolution. In this way, the diver can cover a great deal of area in a fairly short time. Another plus is that he has a good idea of where he is at any given time due to the tether line.

If two divers are available for this search, it is probably best that one remain at the center point and control the amount of line deployed for each revolution, rather than both swimming and controlling the line length at the same time. Also, after a couple of revolutions, one diver can spell the other for a rest break. In order to be truly effective, it is necessary for the search diver to exert some force against the tether line and center point. This is to ensure that all revolutions are fully circular, thus covering all the ground in a uniform manner. The maximum distance out from the center that a diver should search in a circular search pattern is about 100 ft. (30 m). A circle of this radius starts to become a long distance to swim, especially if several circles have already been completed by the same diver. Avoid over-exertion in these and any other diving circumstance.

If this search is unsuccessful, then the center point buoy is left in place and the dive team moves to another adjoining area. These areas should share some overlap to guarantee complete coverage. This process is continued until the entire "high probability" area has been searched. Failure to locate the lost diver will hinge on how well the searches were done and how accurate the original information was. A decision may then be made as to the advisability of moving locations or re-searching the entire area again.

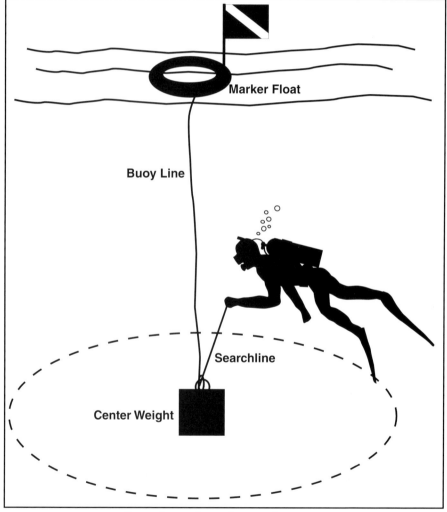

Marker Float

Buoy Line

Searchline

Center Weight

Diver-directed circular search pattern

Sweep search

This is an effective and easily run search technique that can be conducted from a boat or from shore. Usually it is the method of choice in shore-based search situations. The technique requires a tender on shore to direct the diver and deploy search line as required. The diver holds the tending line as he swims in an arc from one side to the other, usually from shallow area to shallow area. Again the diver needs to exert some pull on the line to ensure that all search tracks are parallel and even. As the diver finishes one complete track from shallow to shallow, the tender pays out more line depending on the underwater visibility. Though professionals advise to begin the search

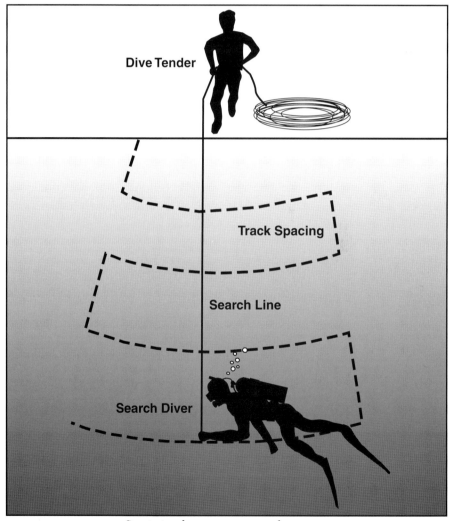

Dive Tender

Track Spacing

Search Line

Search Diver

Semi-circular or sweep search pattern.

at the maximum extent of line and work inwards, most relatively untrained persons find it easier to work out to deeper water. There can be an inherent problem in doing this, since the diver finishes at the farthest distance from shore and in the deepest water. The tender must not let the diver get too far out from shore. Again, the usually-advised maximum distance out will be about 100 ft. (30 m).

The diver and tender both must pay particular attention to underwater features that may snag the search line during the sweeps. Swim high enough above the bottom to avert entanglements, consistent with being able to observe the bottom clearly. Paired divers on the same line works well and permits a greater amount of bottom to be covered in the same time. There is also some comfort in having a second diver along during the tension and stress of a search for a missing fellow diver.

Random searches

There are some circumstances when random searches may have better success than more organized patterns. Along shorelines where there are many rocky outcrops and coves, or where underwater there are crevices and over-hangs, or anywhere the kelp is long and subject to swaying from the surge, the rescue diver may need extra time and the freedom to conduct a more thorough inspection. Regular search patterns rely on the diver running con-sistent and unvarying search tracks to maximize success by ensuring the best coverage. In these difficult search areas, standard patterns will often miss the search object.

Competent free-swimming divers should be deployed to check these fea-tures carefully. Surge can have very unpredictable effects on motionless

Individual divers may be assigned free-swimming roles to run searches in areas not easily examined by standard patterns.

objects and can tuck things in the most unlikely of places. Take the time it takes to do the job fully.

Untended divers need to be watched at all times in these kinds of searches. In a full-blown operation there may be boat traffic overhead, other divers conducting searches in adjacent areas and other auxiliary persons on the scene. The person in charge needs to be fully aware of the location of all search divers in the water at all times.

Abandoning the search

At some stage the search and rescue operation will pass from rescue to a recovery. A rule of thumb is that when an hour and a half has passed after the diver would have run out of air, then survival is unlikely. This takes into account the diver rationing air carefully, but finally succumbing to hypoxia. The period during which we might have hoped for a resuscitation after rescue would be included in this period. Do not endanger other divers by continuing a futile effort. Public safety departments are in a much better position to effect the recovery than most individuals.

Once contact with professional assistance is established by radio, use of cell phones may be preferable. Phones are more private, more secure, and make it easier to communicate complicated plans.

Assisting a diver up to the surface

Finding the missing diver on the bottom or encountering a distressed diver underwater, we need first to determine what the problem is. Be careful not to rush into a situation that you do not fully understand. Your first reaction to solving a problem for another diver may prove to be a solution for a problem that doesn't exist. The correct response to a diver with difficulties underwater will vary depending whether the diver is conscious or unconscious, but always take a second to determine what's really going on.

Conscious diver

Establish contact with the diver while you're still out of arm's reach. Signaling "OK" should provoke some response and will give you an idea of the diver's state of mind. Often the diver will indicate the problem and request some assistance. This might be as simple as a loose weight belt or cramp to more complicated problems like entanglement in fishing line. Before you attempt to lend assistance, however, you should signal the diver your intentions. Sudden movements, however helpful, might disrupt the diver's own attempts to help himself or cause a startle reaction that may not improve the diver's state of mind.

Failure of the diver to respond appropriately to the OK signal probably indicates that the diver requires immediate assistance. We've reviewed many of the problems that divers may experience underwater in Chapter 5. Pay particular attention to the signs of a diver in pain or confusion. Serious hyperbaric issues may be developing and staying on the bottom is probably not an option. The cascade of problems that snowball from little incidents may overwhelm a diver's ability to deal with them. There is probably only one place to solve all these problems in safety, and that is on the surface.

Signal the diver to slow down and take a couple of breaths to relax. This may be only partly successful, but your intention is to escort the diver to the surface and calming him first will aid this. Moving so that the diver can see your approach, gently and firmly grasp him under the arm while signaling to ascend with your other hand. Judge your actions based on what you can see of the diver's reactions. If he fails to vent his BC, you'll have to do this for him as well as for yourself. The diver may try to bolt for the surface or act erratically. Maintain control and continue to signal the diver to relax and breathe normally. Monitor the diver constantly and communicate with him frequently. Just the contact alone sometimes helps a diver keep himself under control.

Ascend at as normal a rate as possible by using good buoyancy control. Weight belts should remain in place unless there is good reason to drop them. A diver may have too little air to spare for inflation or may be seriously over-weighted at depth. If your own BC is inadequate to start you both toward the surface, then it may be appropriate to drop the victim's belt. Understand that this may make control of the ascent in shallow water a problem. Anticipate this by staying ahead of your own buoyancy changes.

Once on the surface, establish positive buoyancy for the victim and your-self. If you determine that his problems are medical rather than gear-related, then drop his weight belt. Signal for help or, if alone, start the swim or tow back to safety. Maintain contact and conversation throughout this time. It's important to talk to the diver. There have been many instances where appar-ently unconscious or otherwise unresponsive divers have been able to recall every word spoken by the rescuer. The effect of human contact on an injured person cannot be overemphasized.

On the shore or boat continue the assessment of the diver's problems. Was there a time when the diver was fully unresponsive? not breathing? out of air underwater? Try to get a history of events from the diver to arrive at cause of the distress. Conduct a neurological exam as outlined in Chapter 6. If there are any signs of neurological impairment or any time that the victim was truly unconscious, immediate medical assistance is necessary.

Unconscious Diver

An unconscious diver on the bottom is in the greatest of peril. If the diver is breathing but unresponsive to our attempts to arouse him, we must escort him to the surface as quickly as we can. Our main concern will be to ascertain that the victim's regulator stays in place on the ascent to safety. There is no uniform position in which a breathing, unconscious scuba diver will rest. Whatever the position, hold the regulator in the victim's mouth while you manipulate him into a posture that will allow you to hold him upright and maintain control of his regulator. The victim is probably nega-tively buoyant at this stage, so drop his weight belt. If in deep water, drop-ping the weight belt by itself may have little effect on the victim's buoyancy, so add a small amount of air to the BC to make him easier to handle.

As you start the ascent, you need to anticipate buoyancy changes in the shallower depths. Venting both BCs will be difficult while sparing a hand for the victim's regulator. If only one BC can be vented, it should be yours. This way you can serve as a brake on the ascent rate, and if you lose the victim, he will continue to ascend. An effort should be made, however, to dump air as you're able from his BC. Without his weight belt and with a BC continu-

Bring a non-breathing diver off the bottom by first removing the weight belt. On a deep dive, it may be necessary to add a little air to the BC to overcome suit compression.

ally filling due to expansion, he may become very difficult to hold down. A complication may be added by a dry suit diver.

Though most dry suit divers also wear a BC, very many, if not most, use the dry suit for buoyancy control. They reserve the BC for emergency use, not for buoyancy control. This means that in order to control the rate of ascent, you will need to purge their suit on ascent. Even if you're familiar with dry suits, this may be difficult to do with one hand. A solution may be to hold the victim from behind so that you can hold the regulator with your right hand and purge the exhaust valve (usually on the diver's left upper arm) with your left.

If the victim is not breathing, waste no time in getting him to the surface. Drop the weight belt, inflate the BC if there is air in the tank and pull him upright. If the regulator is not in his mouth, do not put it back in, you'll only force more water into the lungs. Even in a drowned diver there is still some air in the lungs. Even if there is no appreciable amount of water in the lungs, as may be the case in the early "dry" period of drowning, there is little danger of a lung over-expansion injury. An unconscious person is not holding his breath, thus the expanding air will vent by simple physics on ascent. This may even have the effect of clearing water from the lungs.

Position the victim so you can hold the regulator in their mouth. If the regulator was out of the mouth, do not attempt to replace it.

Bring the diver to the surface as rapidly as possible, but keep in mind your own safety. Depth and/or bottom time may not permit you to ascend quickly. In this case, you may need to let the victim go and recover him again on the surface.

The only caution on ascent with either a breathing or non-breathing victim is your own safety. If ascending from a deep water dive, your nitrogen limits may dictate a slower ascent rate. Remain cognizant of the dangers of a too rapid ascent to your safety. This may result in having to release the victim in shallow water while you stop for decompression or just complete the last 20 ft. (6 m) at a slow rate. Surface conditions may make this last choice a poor option if it's choppy or dark. Finding the victim again may require an agonizing few minutes of searching.

Once at the surface with the victim, drop your own weight belt and add air to the BCs as necessary. This may call for oral inflation of his BC if the victim was out of air. *Shout for help* and prepare to start in-water rescue breathing, as described in Chapter 4.

When dropping your own or a buddy's weight belt, be sure to hold it away from the body as you let go of it. Falling belts can snag on buckles or tools as they fall.

Scuba I.Q. Review

1. What kinds of information do we need to gather to plan an underwater search?

2. List the three major components in any underwater search pattern.

3. When might we use free-swimming divers to conduct random searches?

4. How would you bring a conscious, but confused diver to the surface?

5. If the diver is breathing, but unresponsive on the bottom, what would our main concern be as we bring him to the surface?

6. Why is a lung over-expansion injury not a serious consideration when bringing an unconscious, non-breathing victim to the surface?

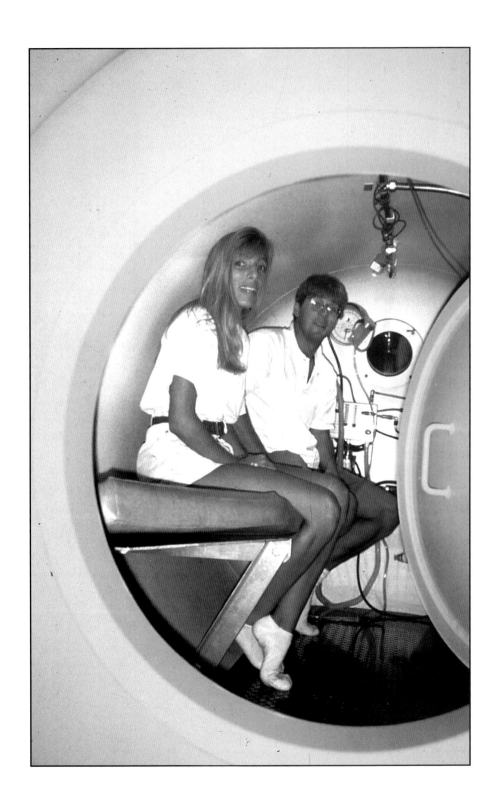

Chapter 8
Recompression
Chambers and Therapy

Why recompression?

Dive accidents that involve the formation of bubbles in the blood and body tissues are usually caused by decompression incidents. Specifically, the injuries occur because of a drop in ambient pressure as the diver ascends toward the surface. As we have seen already, these barotraumas fall into two major groups, decompression sickness and lung over-expansion injuries.

We also know that good, on-scene first aid will include the delivery to the patient of as high a concentration of pure oxygen as we can manage. The O_2 may help to reduce bubble size and get some oxygen through diffusion to tissues cut off from direct circulation by bubbles. Still, bubbles will persist, and even continue to grow over time, which accounts for the progressive nature of decompression sickness. Left on their own, little bubbles often get bigger, causing greater and greater damage.

In the case of DCS, nitrogen dissolved in the blood and tissues pops out of solution to form micro-bubbles. This happens when the diver ascends too quickly (decompresses) and the excess nitrogen is not given sufficient time to be safely exhaled. In the case of "free" air in the body and circulation from a lung rupture, the diver ascended while holding his breath. This air, too, expands as the ascent continues and the diver continues to decompress until reaching the surface.

In both cases, gases were released from pressure and allowed to expand in the body. Clearly, the smaller the bubbles can be made after the fact, the less pain and damage will result. It makes sense, then, to subject the diver to pressure again to shrink the bubbles to the smallest size possible. If we could shrink the bubbles sufficiently, we could drive them into solution and resolve these illnesses. This is why we use recompression chambers in the event of major barotraumas.

Decompression stops and safety stops are the best way to avoid decompression sickness. These planned stops allow our bodies to unload excess nitrogen and to minimize the formation of bubbles in the circulation and body tissues.

Recompression and decompression chambers

Chambers used to pressurize divers come in a variety of sizes and types, but divers are not the only group treated in a hyperbaric environment. Many large hospitals now use chambers to treat a spectrum of illnesses and diseases including burns, carbon monoxide poisoning, and even migraines. These are large walk-in facilities resembling ward rooms. The benefits of hyperbaric oxygen have long been recognized and are increasingly studied for application in other treatment regimes including multiple sclerosis. For the diver, the benefits include both hyperbaric oxygen and the direct effects of pressure.

There is no physical difference between a "recompression chamber" and a "decompression chamber." They are built to the same specifications, the American Society of Mechanical Engineers (ASME) code known as "PVHO," i.e., Pressure Vessel for Human Occupancy. The only distinction between a recompression chamber and decompression chamber is the application or use of the chamber. The more appropriate term would be "hyperbaric chamber."

Decompression chambers are the staple of the working deep water diver. Spending a working day in depths of 300-500 ft. (90-150 m), these divers would require very long decompression obligations to surface safely. Entering double-lock chambers at or near their working depths, the chambers are lifted on board support vessels where the divers can complete their decompression schedules in a warm and dry environment. In fact, there are live-in, onboard chambers where divers can spend their non-working hours in comfort and then be lowered in similar chambers to the working depth again for the next day's work. In this way the divers remain "saturated" with the inert gases of their breathing mixtures and may incur no more decompression time than if they'd spent only a day on the bottom. This is far more efficient and safer for the diver, than fully decompressing and then fully recompressing the next day.

Recompression chambers are most often used to repressurize a diver, in other words to return him to equivalent depth without putting him back in the water. Most chambers are similar in form, large cylinders on their side with hatch doors for entry. They range in size from one-man units with as little as a 36 inch (about 1 m) entry port, to multi-person chambers with room for 4 divers and a dive medic attendant. Many small models are designed and equipped for field use and are fully portable. These units are manufactured by several companies around the world and are frequently used for remote commercial and serious technical diving activities where other facilities are scarce or non-existent.

Some decompression chambers are large enough for several divers and dive medics.

Diving is simulated by pumping pressurized air into the chamber and, thereby, increasing the ambient pressure. Pressure increases simulate diving deeper until the desired "depth" is reached. Throughout this "descent," the diver experiences the same pressure changes as descending underwater, i. e., ears must be cleared, and any sinus problems the diver might have underwater will be evident in the chamber. The chamber becomes increasingly heated, too, from the compressing air, and ventilation becomes an issue with the deeper dives. Interestingly, voice sounds change as the compressed, denser air transmits sounds much faster, raising the pitch of the voice. This can be a very disconcerting phenomenon to those who haven't experienced this before!

The chamber operator monitors the internal pressure, temperature and air purity on gauges on the outside of the chamber. An intercom or telephone is used to communicate from the outside, where a hyperbaric physician may direct the treatment, to the inside. The dive medic monitors the patient carefully for pressure-related problems, as well as taking and recording frequent vital sign checks. In addition to being returned to a hyperbaric environment whose purpose is to shrink the offending bubbles, the diver will also be put on a pure oxygen breathing medium. This hastens bubble removal and reoxygenates ischemic tissue.

To avoid building up an oxygen-rich environment inside the chamber, however, with its associated fire hazards, the diver breathes the O_2 through a mask. Oxygen is supplied by the operator only when the patient uses the mask. Hyperbaric oxygen has the side-effect of causing nervous system reactions such as convulsions and paralysis. As such, patients are monitored closely for the signs and symptoms of oxygen toxicity during the chamber episode. The dive medic will typically cycle the patient on and off oxygen for periods of time to avoid serious complications while still promoting its benefits.

Recompression therapy

Divers are recompressed according to preset tables which guide the treatment period. Though depths and times vary in some instances, the general rule has become that serious DCS events are immediately returned to the equivalent of 60 ft. (18 m) where oxygen therapy is begun in an "on- off again" cycle. In some extreme instances of DCI, injured divers may even be brought down as deep as 165 ft. (50 m) or 6 ATA (atmospheres absolute). Many patients experience immediate relief from symptoms as this therapy is begun. This is in fact the only true verification that the signs and symptoms thus far exhibited by the patient are actual DCS.

There are numerous stories of remarkable recoveries of critically injured divers in recompression chambers. In some instances, divers in full cardiac arrest have spontaneously re-established a heart rhythm. The treatment continues through progressively shallower depths until the patient is returned to the "surface," a process that may take 4 hours or more. If the patient is lucky, the hyperbaric accident has now run its course and pains will not recur. Note, however, that some cases are not easily cleared up and may require several chamber dives to resolve. Some of these dives may be much longer than the original recompression and become very burdensome. This is especially true in cases where the time after the initial diving incident that precipitated the bends symptoms and when the patient presents himself for treatment is lengthy.

There is no doubt that the earlier treatment is begun, the easier symptoms are to resolve. This argues strongly that all divers should be familiar with the field signs and symptoms of DCI so that on-scene treatment can be begun and transport arranged for the afflicted diver as soon as possible. A final sobering note: many divers redevelop symptoms that may persist for months afterwards, even after several treatments. The rescue diver needs to know what to look for and how to respond appropriately.

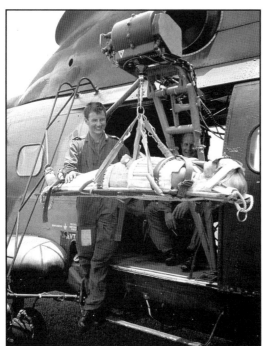

Helicopter evacuation from remote dive areas to definitive medical care may be an option. Part of your dive planning should include determining the level of emergency resources available.

Chapter 8

Divers, do you know where your chambers are?

Few divers give much thought to the processes of rescue and emergency response to a dive accident until it happens. We've learned that preparation is always the best hedge against the unforeseen, and so we seek to become qualified rescue divers. The rescue doesn't end on the beach, however, and we may well need to know exactly where to transport the victim for definitive care. This will vary from one place to another. In some instances help will come directly to you and relieve you of lifesaving responsibilities. In other areas you may need to transport to a recompression chamber yourself.

Bear in mind that even if you are certain that the victim will require recompression because you determined beyond a doubt that a lung over-expansion injury has occurred or that decompression sickness is the culprit, you may *not* be permitted to transport the victim directly to the chamber facility. *Local protocol may insist that any diving patient first be transported to a medical facility for evaluation.* The attending physician may then recommend recompression therapy. Part of our preparation, then, is to obtain the sure knowledge of the appropriate manner of action to minimize confusion and delay in the event of an accident.

Traveling to and diving in an unfamiliar area means, among other things, finding out in advance what services are available and how to access them. There will likely be some noteworthy differences between what you're used to and how things are done here. You may decide as a precaution to minimize the exposure of your dives if the lack of ready assistance warrants it. To find out how the local system is activated, inquire at a local dive shop, talk to other divers in the area and call an area hospital before you finish planning for the dive trip. There are online sources available, too. For example, a list of recompression chambers and associated diving physicians worldwide can be found at the web site www.gulftel.com. Some diving agencies also offer information on area chambers through their web sites, or can be contacted directly for further guidance.

It's clear that recompression may be the one procedure that can save a diver's life in some instances. Even if a chamber is nearby and accessible, however, this treatment, along with the expenses associated with an evacuation, is not inexpensive. Insurance developed specifically for scuba divers is available and very worthwhile. TDI/SDI DiveSafe insurance is an example of worldwide coverage that offers you protection from devastating air evacuation and recompression chambers costs.

Scuba I.Q. Review

1. What is the value of recompression in decompression sickness accidents?

2. What is the difference between decompression chambers and recompression chambers?

3. How does a chamber simulate descending to depth?

4. Do you know where the nearest chamber is to your frequent dive sites?

Appendix

A Diver's First Aid Kit

TDI/SDI recommends that all divers obtain training in first aid and oxygen therapy. For rescue divers this is particularly important as they may be the most qualified lifesavers on the accident scene. Below is a suggested list of contents for a diver's first aid kit:

First aid manual
TDI/SDI CPROX manual
Oxygen kit with selection of appropriate masks
Disposable latex or vinyl surgical gloves
Barrier mask for CPR
2 liters of fluid; 1 liter of a sport drink for electrolyte replacement, I liter of water
Topical disinfectant such as Betadine for barnacle and coral scrapes
Topical antibiotic cream for cuts and scrapes
Topical anesthetic or anti-itch cream
50% hydrogen peroxide, an effective external ear wash
Eye drops to wash out foreign objects
Decongestant tablets such as Sudafed to drain blocked sinuses or ears after diving
Antihistamine tablets such as Chlor-Trimeton to reduce swelling and irritation in ears and sinuses
Eye dropper
Gauze squares, 4"x 4", for use as pressure bandages to stop bleeding
Absorbent pads for bleeding
Assortment of 'bandaids'
Self-adhesive surgical dressing to cover large wounds

Tweezers, scissors, sharp knife or scalpel
Air-activated heat pads
Cold packs to reduce swelling of sprains
Reflective 'Space Blanket' for wrapping cold persons
Plastic bag for the disposal of soiled or blood-contaminated items
Notebook and pen to record information

Useful contact information:

DAN (Divers Alert Network) (919) 684-2948
This is a 24-hour hot line for information and advice on the treatment of diving injuries.
US Coast Guard Monitors VHF Channel 16 continuously.
Also can be reached locally via telephone or cellular phone. Obtain the phone number for your area.

Blood-Borne Pathogens

The possibility of transmission of disease organisms from one person to another is heightened by contact with body fluids. While that possibility is greatest through contact with another person's blood, mucus and other fluids may also carry viruses and bacteria. Of greatest concern is the accidental transmission of HIV and hepatitis viruses. Despite the fear of contracting these disease agents, transmission in the aquatic environment during rescue operations is very remote. The sharing of regulators, for example, has never been shown to transmit HIV or hepatitis. The marine environment is patently hostile to HIV, although hepatitis A will survive in both salt and fresh water. Although transmission during in-water resuscitation efforts would be unlikely, caution is advised.

Dry land rescue procedures, especially first aid, however, does carry a greater risk of accidental infection. The first aid provider should avoid contacting the body fluids of another person by using disposable surgical gloves during treatment of actively bleeding wounds. Wash off any contaminating body fluids as soon as possible after exposure to your skin or clothing. One-way valve barrier masks are recommended for CPR on land.

"Universal precautions" as a means of reducing the transmission of causative agents of disease is included in many modern first aid courses and should be a matter of standard practice for all responders.

About the Author- Joe Mokry

Joe's interest and involvement in water rescue, particularly scuba rescue, has been direct and long-standing. As a diving instructor for more than 15 years, Joe has been instrumental in developing new techniques and strategies for rescue, and delivered these to hundreds of students in training classes. This resulted in his being awarded NAUI's annual Outstanding Service Award. Now as an Instructor Trainer for TDI/SDI, he is passing along this knowledge to new instructor-candidates.

Joe's background includes a Master of Biology, Wilderness EMT, First Aid and CPR instructor, and oxygen-therapy instructor. A licensed Able Bodied Seaman and Coast Guard certified Ship's Master, Joe is most at home on, in or under the ocean. His long association with marine rescue led to his developing a Fast Rescue Boats program that has been certified by the US Coast Guard and recognized by the International Maritime Organization, one of only a half-dozen such programs world-wide that has reached this level of distinction. A working, professional diver himself, his work with Public Safety departments in all aspects of water rescue, including Dive Rescue Team training and Search and Recovery Team training routinely takes him across the country as a trainer and speaker. Two of his more esoteric specialties are training "high exposure" Rescue Swimmers and Fast Rescue Craft crews for the extremes of rescue situations.

A Maine resident, Joe spends much of his time as a Visiting Professor at the Massachusetts Maritime Academy on Cape Cod where he trains both cadets and maritime professionals in international-standard courses. As a long-serving member and officer of the Cape Elizabeth Water Extrication Team (WETeam), he has received several commendations for rescue operations, including the prestigious Public Service Commendation for his actions in the rescue of a downed Air-Med helicopter pilot in horrendous sea conditions.

Joe can be reached through Ocean Rescue Systems at www.oceanrescue.com.

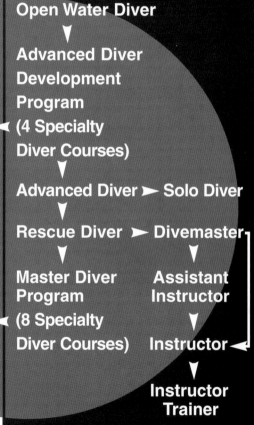

SDI DIVER PROGRAMS

SCUBA DIVING INTERNATIONAL

Open Water Diver
▼
Advanced Diver Development Program
(4 Specialty Diver Courses)
▼
Advanced Diver ► Solo Diver
▼
Rescue Diver ► Divemaster
▼   ▼
Master Diver Program   Assistant Instructor
(8 Specialty Diver Courses)   ▼
                     Instructor
                     ▼
                     Instructor Trainer

- Altitude Diver
- Boat Diver
- Computer Diver
- Computer Nitrox Diver
- CPROX Administrator
- CPR1st Administrator
- Deep Diver(130ft Max)
- Diver Propulsion Vehicle
- Drift Diver
- Dry Suit Diver
- Equipment Specialist
- Ice Diver
- Marine Ecosystems Awareness
- Night/ Limited Visibility Diver
- Research Diver
- Search & Recovery Diver
- Shore/Beach Diver
- Underwater Navigation
- Underwater Photography
- Underwater Video
- Wreck Diver
- Underwater Hunter & Collector

Glossary

After-drop: Continued cooling of the body core of a hypothermic victim after rewarming. Too rapid external rewarming can cause a catastrophic core temperature drop and cardiac arrest.

AGE: See arterial gas embolism

Alveolus: Air sac at the very end of lung passages. Plural is alveoli.

Amnesia: Loss of memory.

Arterial gas embolism: Bubble of air trapped in the arterial side of the circulation causing a blockage of blood flow. Possible result of a lung over-expansion injury.

Artery: Blood vessel that carries blood away from the heart.

Aspiration: Inhaling foreign matter into the lungs, such as vomit

Barnacle : Marine animal which attaches to a firm substrate such as rock and is characterized by a hard, sharp volcano-shaped shell.

Barotrauma: Injury caused by changes in pressure.

Bends: Popular term for decompression sickness.

Breath trigger: Elevated level of carbon dioxide in the circulating blood that stimulates the breathing response.

Bronchitis: Excessive mucus or other fluid production in the lungs resulting in chronic cough.

Capillary: Tiny blood vessels through which oxygen and carbon dioxide are exchanged across the lung tissue and other organs.

Carabiner: Spring-loaded clip for connecting lines, harnesses or hardware.

Carbon dioxide: Gas produced in the body from the combustion of oxygen and organic materials. Odorless, colorless and tasteless.

Carbon monoxide: Toxic gas produced from the incomplete combustion of oxygen and organic materials. Odorless, colorless and tasteless.

Cardiac arrest: Sudden stopping of cardiac output resulting in loss of a pulse.

Cardiovascular fitness: A measure of overall capacity to perform at a sustained level of exercise; a measure of endurance.

Carotid artery: Artery that supplies the head and brain with blood. Pulse from these two arteries can be felt on either side of the Adam's apple.

Carotid sinus reflex: Reaction of the circulation to disproportionate pressure being applied to the carotid artery, resulting in drop in blood pressure and flow to the brain. Usually leads to blackout.

Conduction: Transfer of heat from one source to another by direct contact.

Convection: Loss of heat from a body caused by air or water flow across its surface.

Current reversal (eddy): Change in direction of water flow caused by an obstruction in the water course.

Cyanosis: Blue tinge to skin and nail beds resulting from poor or no oxygen supply.

DCI: See decompression illness.

DCS: See decompression sickness.

Decompression chamber: A pressurized air chamber used to permit deep water divers to return to normal atmospheric pressure while out of the water. Mechanically identical to a recompression chamber. More properly referred to as a "hyperbaric chamber."

Decompression illness: Term used to describe the major barotraumas in diving and includes decompression sickness and lung over-expansion injuries.

Decompression sickness: Condition caused by the expansion of nitrogen bubbles in the body tissues during or following an ascent, especially in the connective tissues of the joints.

Glossary

Dorsal fin: Prominent fin on the back of a fish.

Drowning: Suffocation caused by the inhalation of water.

Dysfunction: Inability to function properly.

Embolism: Blockage in circulation caused by bubbles, blood clots or other matter.

Free flow: An event where the regulator delivers air constantly. May be caused by ice formation within the moving parts, or because of inadequate servicing.

Freeze up: An event where the regulator stops supplying air due to an ice blockage in the first stage.

Global awareness: Consciousness and perception of one's surroundings.

Hemoglobin: Protein in blood cells which is responsible for carrying oxygen and carbon dioxide.

Hydraulic: Term used to describe the circulating water flow that forms down-stream of a submerged object in a current.

Hyperthermia: Elevated core temperature due to the body's inability to cool properly.

Hypothermia: Lowered core temperature due to the body's inability produce and conserve heat as quickly as it is lost.

Hypovolemic shock: Failure of circulation to supply oxygen to the body tis-sues due to lack of sufficient fluids.

Hypoxia: Lack of sufficient oxygen

Ischemia: Lack of blood supply to body tissues resulting in a lack of oxygen.

Knots: Measure of speed, one nautical mile (6076 ft.) per hour or about 1.1 statute (land) mile per hour or about 1.8 kilometers per hour.

Longshore current: Ocean current running parallel to shore , usually set up by tides or persistent winds and surf.

Lowhead dam: Manmade structure across a river which holds back flow at low water levels, but permits overflow at times of high water.

Mediastinal emphysema: Gathering of air into the space between the two lungs surrounding the heart, major blood vessels, and trachea. A possible consequence of a lung over-expansion injury and rupture.

Nasal cannula: An oxygen-delivery device consisting of plastic tubes that drape around the patient's head and end in short tabs that release oxygen directly into the nostrils.

Nematocyst: Specialized cells possessed by jellyfish and other stinging invertebrates which contain tiny harpoon-like devices used for defense and food gathering.

Neurotoxic venom: Poisonous fluid injected by sea snakes and other animals having its principle effect on the nervous system.

Nitrogen narcosis: Stuporous or elated state induced by the narcotic effect of nitrogen on the body. Associated with relatively deep diving.

Oxygen toxicity: A possibly life-threatening condition characterized by convulsions, caused by breathing oxygen at elevated partial pressures.

Panic: Overwhelming fear and loss of self-control in the face of real or imagined danger.

Panting: Abnormal breathing pattern characterized by rapid, shallow breaths, resulting in elevated carbon dioxide levels, hypoxia and the feeling of suffocation.

Pectoral fin: Fin located just below and behind the gills on a fish.

Plasma: The portion of blood that is liquid and non-cellular.

Pleural membranes: Membranes covering the lungs and inside of the chest wall.

Pneumothorax: Free air between pleural membranes. A possible consequence of a ruptured lung, and may lead to a collapsed lung.

Primary survey: Initial assessment conducted to detect and correct life-threatening medical conditions.

Recompression chamber   A pressurized air chamber used to simulate returning a diver to depth for the treatment of major barotraumas. Mechanically identical to a decompression chamber. More properly referred to as a "hyperbaric chamber."

Red blood cells: The major cellular component of blood that carries oxygen.

Rescue: The removal of a person from danger.

Respiratory arrest: Cessation of breathing.

Resuscitation: Act of reviving an unconscious or apparently dead person.

Reverse block (or squeeze): A condition where high pressure air is trapped in the middle ear or sinus, causing discomfort or pain on ascent.

Rip: Relatively high velocity stream of water moving directly away from shore, usually set up by deflected longshore currents or dammed tidal waters.

Secondary survey: Assessment of the patient undertaken to detect problems that are not immediately life-threatening, but which may become more serious if left untreated.

Self-awareness: Consciousness of one's own feelings and perceptions; being alert.

Sign: An observable indication of the patient's condition, such as shivering or cyanosis.

Skip-breathing: An abnormal and deliberate breathing pattern alteration characterized by brief breath-holding followed by a prolonged exhalation and then repeated. The intent is to obtain more bottom time from a scuba cylinder, but often results in hypoxia and severe headache.

Sprain: Injury involving tearing or stretching of ligaments.

Squeeze: A direct effect of pressure on air spaces in the body or beneath equipment next to the body in response to increased pressure on descent.

Stress: A physical and emotional challenge to an individual requiring some effort to maintain control and mental balance.

Stroke: Sudden loss of neurological function due to interruption of blood flow to some part of the brain.

Subcutaneous emphysema: The presence of air directly under the skin which may have migrated from other parts of the body. A possible consequence of a lung over-expansion injury.

Supine: Lying flat on one's back.

Surge: Back and forth motion of water associated with the passage of a swell.

Symptom: An indication of the patient's condition that he feels and describes.

Thoracic cavity: The space in the chest occupied by the lungs, trachea and esophagus.

Trachea: Windpipe

Tuberculosis: Bacterial disease affecting the lungs and other body parts. Spread by coughing and sneezing (droplet dispersal).

Type I bends: Symptoms of decompression sickness principally characterized by joint pains and skin rash or itch.

Type II bends: Very serious form of decompression sickness caused by growth of nitrogen bubbles in the spinal cord and elsewhere. Symptoms include 'pins and needles' in the legs, radiating back and abdominal pain, weakness in legs and paralysis.

Vein: Blood vessel that carries blood back towards the heart.

Venous gas embolism: Nitrogen bubbles collected in the veins as the gas comes out of solution and the tissues on ascent.

Visualization: Act of producing a set of mental images related to an impending activity or event for the purpose of preparing emotionally and mentally for the activity.

Index

A

abdomen 147, 150
abdominal pain 82
abrasions 136
absorbent bandage 136
absorbent dressing 61
accident 36, 45, 60, 64, 66, 105, 106, 128, 129, 139, 140, 158, 179
accident prevention 106
accident rate 45, 51
Adam's apple 152, 155
adaptation 112
adipose tissue 122
after-drop 156
AGE 153
air 25, 31, 49, 57, 84, 85, 87, 106, 116, 171
air consumption 18, 35
air cylinder 17
air donor 22
air evacuation 184
air pressure 20, 22, 58
air sac 125
air space 59, 114, 118
air starvation 40, 42
air supply 20, 24, 83
air testing 111
airway 25, 82, 87, 88, 94, 133, 146, 147, 153, 155, 157
alcohol 113, 122, 135
allergy 117
Alpha flag 60, 61
alternate air source 24

alveoli 125, 126, 128
ambient pressure 25, 125, 179
American Red Cross 46
ammonia 135
amnesia 113
anchor 106
anchor line 51, 107
ankle injury 61
annual gear inspection 17
anti-venin 133
antibiotic cream 136
antihistamines 117, 135
anxiety 31, 39, 41, 42
apprehension 31, 33, 34, 42, 113
argon 112
arterial gas embolism 125, 128, 129
ascent 18, 25, 113, 116, 121, 125, 127, 173, 174, 176, 179
ascent rate 27, 121
aspiration 87
assist 69
assistance 14, 24, 27, 47, 172

B

back 88, 89, 99, 101
backboard 94
backup air supply 20
baking soda 135
balance 151
balance mechanism 115
bandages 61, 132
barnacles 135
barotrauma 82, 83, 120, 179